BUSINESS FUNDAMENTALS:

HOW TO BECOME A SUCCESSFUL BUSINESS MAN

BUSINESS FUNDAMENTALS:

How to Become a Successful Business Man

Roger W. Babson

COSIMO CLASSICS

NEW YORK

Cosimo, P.O. Box 416
Old Chelsea Station
New York, NY 10113-0416

or visit our website at:
www.cosimobooks.com

BUSINESS FUNDAMENTALS: How to Become a Successful Business Man originally published by B.C. Forbes Publishing Company in 1923.

Library of Congress Cataloging-in-Publication Data

A catalog record for this book is available from the Library of Congress

Cover design by www.wiselephant.com

ISBN: 1-59605-639-8

TABLE OF CONTENTS

CHAPTER I

CHAPTER II

CHAPTER III

CHAPTER IV

INTRODUCTION TO REVISED EDITION

THOUGH written five years ago, "Business Fundamentals" continues in constant demand and the publishers have asked me to prepare this complete revision. The statistics and charts have been brought up to date and new material has been added. In each chapter the necessary revisions have been made so that all statements and forecasts are from the viewpoint of today. I have written an entirely new chapter: "A Continuous Working Plan For Your Money."

In reviewing the five years that have elapsed, I am more than ever impressed with two facts. First: business and financial conditions are continually and rapidly changing, like pictures on a movie film. Second: fundamentals such as the law of action and reaction are forever permanent; they are the same today as they were five years ago, and they will remain the same for five million years to come.

R. W. B.

BABSON PARK, MASS.
OCTOBER, 1927.

BUSINESS FUNDAMENTALS

CHAPTER I

THE USE OF STATISTICS

STATISTICS, as far as we are concerned, will be understood to represent concentrated information reduced to the exact basis of figures. This gives us a tremendous field. Since, however, we are interested only in the statistics which affect business and investments, we will discard the rest and concentrate on this particular branch. These figures are divided into two distinct classes — comparative statistics and fundamental statistics.

Comparative statistics, such as would concern the merchant, for instance, relate to weight, quality, age, and method of manufacture of the merchandise in which he deals, together with such trade figures as are published in trade journals. Under this heading are also grouped the figures that appear on the merchant's books — the figures that represent the inside condition of his particular business. From the investor's point of view, comparative statistics include all particulars concerning the bonded debt, earnings, gross business, and financial condition of a given property. They reflect inside conditions.

These figures are very necessary to bankers and investors for comparing similar securities of different companies and different securities of the same company.

Fundamental statistics, on the other hand, reveal the broad general situation that affects every one. These underlying conditions, such as supply and demand, are of tremendous importance because they affect a man's business *fundamentally*. They govern the purchasing power of his customers, the price of the raw materials he uses, and the living conditions of the workers in his plant.

The importance of comparative statistics is generally accepted and understood. Hence, business men now freely spend much money for bookkeepers, accountants, and office assistants to record the necessary data. Nearly every business compiles them to a certain extent, and most concerns employ from 10 to 50 per cent. of their office forces on this work.

Few business men, on the other hand, make any systematic effort to collect data and study fundamental statistics. Those who have taken pains to do so are conspicuous in their own business community for their unusual prosperity and what their friends call " good luck." The reason is this: *fundamental statistics are more important to the business man than those reflected in the figures on his own books, for fundamental conditions have more to do with his success.*

An investigation by Professor David Friday, formerly of the Economics Department of the University of Michigan, now head of the State School of Agriculture, revealed the more or less astonishing fact that the largest portion of business profits and losses results from changes in fundamental conditions. A more recent investigation made by my associates, covering over 400 concerns representing the twenty-six leading branches of industry, revealed that 57 per cent. of business profit is the result of changes in fundamental conditions, while but 43 per cent. is the result of competitive efficiency.

The absolute necessity of keeping records and compiling comparative statistics within the individual business is already recognized and has been adopted in general practice. The present problem among business men and investors is how to tie up their internal records of an individual industry or concern with the external statistics of industry as a whole. We will, therefore, henceforward confine ourselves almost exclusively to a discussion of fundamental statistics and possibilities of profit, both in the business field and in the investment markets.

Past financial history has consisted of distinct phases, and, although of different durations, each phase has usually consisted of four periods: (1) a period of prosperity, (2) a period of decline, (3) a period of depression, (4) a period of improvement. These always follow one another in the same sequence and cause a constant change of surface conditions with which one must reckon.

Theoretically, there should be a state where everybody is busy, and nobody overtrades; where the cost of living is reasonable, and the wage earner has a chance to save for old age and to establish a higher standard of comfort. As it is, however, conditions are constantly changing; prices are going up or coming down; the wage that afforded a comfortable living in 1914 will hardly pay the rent today; orders come in bunches, so that the manufacturer is either worked to death trying to get the goods out or is rushing around feverishly to get enough orders to keep his plant running. The average business man, the victim of these circumstances, is going it blind and is bound to lose.

Common sense dictates that, as long as conditions keep changing and are bound to continue to do so, the first step is that of defense.

The business man must have up-to-the-minute facts on current conditions in every part of his field of activity. He must know just how things stand; so that his decision may apply to the situation as it is. For this purpose he must use fundamental statistics. Such statistics must be collected from many sources. The government departments at Washington are especially helpful, supplying much valuable data on conditions at regular intervals. Special commissions, from time to time, investigate fundamental conditions in one field or another and issue enlightening reports. Then there are the special libraries, public libraries, questionnaires, personal correspondence, trade publications, trade association reports, clipping bureaus, surveys and special reports in the field.

The constant changes in fundamental conditions, which harass and befuddle the average business man, offer a remarkable opportunity for profit, provided one can tell *what* the next change will be and *when* it will take place. These two factors will be discussed in succeeding chapters; but, before we close this discussion of statistics and their possibilities, let us consider the dollar-and-cents value of the time spent in studying them. *The amount of money that can be made by the study of such statistics is limited only by the original capital and the number of years the study is continued.*

Comparative statistics treat of comparative conditions and are used for selecting securities and commodities that are fundamentally sound and that have the greatest prospect of increase in market value under existing market conditions. Fundamental statistics treat of underlying conditions and are employed for determining these general market conditions and whether or not it is wise to purchase, or to sell, or to do neither. Investors use these data to guide them in purchasing securities only when they are low, holding them for a time until they are high, and then selling them and keeping the funds liquid in a bank account or in short-term securities. They keep the money thus liquid until the same securities again sell low, when they once more purchase the same or other sound securities.

Many such investors double their money every few years, with practically no risk and with very little trouble. By a study of these fundamental statistics, with little risk and without any purchases on margin, it has been possible to purchase outright, high grade, dividend paying securities such as are included in the Dow-Jones averages, to have turned an investment of about $6,000 into over $600,000 in less than thirty-five years, as shown in Chapter XV. When one realizes the meaning of this — that an investment could have been increased to 100 times its original size within an investment lifetime — the value of fundamental statistics is apparent.

If one is not strictly an investor and is willing, under a broker's guidance, to take advantage also of certain intermediate movements which come once or twice a year, greater profits are sometimes obtained. But, of course, this latter method involves risk. Such operations are not based on statistics.

Many brokers urge customers to take advantage of declines, recommending short selling in periods of great activity and prosperity and also purchasing on margin during periods of depression. But short selling and margin purchasing involve other elements of risk, and the investor taking such risks becomes a *gambler*.

The point, however, that this book would emphasize is that a knowledge of fundamental conditions will enable the business man to increase materially his profits in any business without the risks involved in ordinary speculation. The same information will enable the investor to multiply an original investment of a thousand dollars to a very sizable estate in sound securities with very little risk and without marginal purchases or short sales. The requisites are a constant study of comparative and fundamental statistics and sufficient *self-control* to act only in accordance with what those statistics clearly indicate and to listen neither to the optimism nor pessimism supplied by the daily papers and by the many individuals who are always giving free advice.

The above principles apply to bonds as truly as to stocks, and should be studied by the investors who purchase only bonds, as well as those who purchase stocks. Although bonds do not fluctuate so widely as stocks and for this reason do not present so great an opportunity for profit, yet the minimum interest yield of good bonds is definitely fixed, which is not true of even the most conservative stocks. Bonds are especially recommended to persons dependent upon the income derived from their investments. Furthermore, the writer is inclined to advise that *all persons should always have a portion of their principal on deposit in a bank, or in high-grade bonds, short-term notes, or commercial paper.*

Merchants who never buy or sell securities use these data with equal profit. Fundamental statistics clearly show the merchant when to buy and increase his stock of goods, and when to cut prices and reduce his stock. They also enable the merchant to forecast money conditions in order that he may intelligently decide whether to borrow, to allow customers further credit, or to reduce his loans and the indebtedness of his customers. Moreover, at all times, these figures show the merchant the condition of business throughout the country; so that he knows whether the growth or contraction of his business is proportional to that of competitors.

Upon careful thought, it must be admitted that the fortunes of American merchant princes must have been created by a knowledge of these facts, rather than simply selling to the trade at a nominal profit. Therefore, the proper use of fundamental statistics not only insures a merchant against losses, but should also be as profitable to him as to the investor.

Not only do students of fundamental statistics make large fortunes for themselves and their followers, but such students are the very best patriots a country can produce. The true patriot is he who studies fundamental statistics and who acts in accordance with what they teach, buying very heavily during the days of panic and great depression. The real traitor today is he who urges on or follows the crowd during a period of over-expansion, and then locks up his money and refuses to extend aid during the dark days when banks are failing, railroads are becoming bankrupt, and the wheels of industry are stopping.

Therefore, every additional person who enters into this work will aid in making the next period of over-expansion less riotous and the next depression less severe. He will perform a real service by helping to eliminate unemployment, business failures and social distress.

Chapter II

FUNDAMENTALS AND WHAT
THEY FORETELL

I HAVE already defined comparative and fundamental statistics. A study of the latter reveals the exact condition of the country at any given time, and also — by application of the law of action and reaction — the trend of business. The business man may study hundreds of pages of data and spend vast quantities of time and money in business, but if he does not have the fundamental facts he is like a small boat on the ocean when the storm comes.

It is necessary, of course, to go into exhaustive research on matters pertaining to one's line of business. Only those who are doing this in the most thorough manner have made a success. But this study alone is not sufficient; men who have pursued this policy have become very wealthy, only to lose everything in a few months simply because they did not know fundamentals. They did not know that their own business was dependent upon the general trend of economic conditions. When the fundamentals changed — fundamentals which were sure to affect all business — they did not know it and were caught napping. I have often seen an entire business, the result of the accumulation of years, collapse like a house of cards.

Some years ago I made an investigation of one hundred leading industries to see if they had any special secret of success. I soon found that there was no particular group which had a distinct advantage over the other groups. Nor was heredity, environment, education, or any other such helpful factor sufficient to make the great difference between failure and success. It is true that certain fundamentals of character were necessary, but I became convinced that character alone was not enough. It was evident that the outstanding factor which marked the success of these great captains of industry was their *methods of operation.*

Not content with having a large group of engineers and experts continually investigating along the lines of their respective industries, they also had statistical departments which continually laid before them the trends of all the leading trade indicators. By such investigation they could at all times be reasonably sure of the direction in which business as a whole was traveling.

Unlike their competitors, they refused to " guess." They studied the fundamental statistics of the country. They believed what Colonel Ayres, vice-president of the Cleveland Trust Company, has stated so pertinently to the business men of the country:

"The most important single piece of business information that the man of affairs can have is that which tells him at what stage of the changing course of business he is at any given time."

There are a large number of subjects which should be studied in order to gauge the situation correctly, but the sifting process of years has reduced the number which are of practical and definite use for the business man. In selecting these, the following characteristics are necessary: (1) comprehensive and authoritative figures on the desired subject must be obtainable; (2) the figures must extend over a sufficient number of years to show the business trend. This process of selection has given us some thirty or more subjects on which reliable data for the study of business trends in the United States can be obtained.

A fundamental subject is one which shows, to some degree, the underlying conditions of the country. The keenest and most successful merchants and investors have for years studied such subjects, thereby eliminating losses and making very large profits, as the business seasons have rolled around.

Some years ago I was on a trip to England interviewing the great merchants and other successful business men of that famous trading country. I discussed with them at length the comparative data and current positions of leading corporations.

" This is all very well and quite essential," said they at last, " but what we want and what the mercantile world wants is to know how the United States is headed. We buy your railroads, your mines and your industrials — everything is booming. We turn our backs for a moment, and everything has plunged into a cataclysm. If you will study the fundamentals over there as we study them here, you can perform a most wonderful service."

That set me thinking; I began an investigation of the available information and after months of research selected and arranged the statistics on certain important subjects, the number of which has gradually been enlarged. Some of the important ones are as follows:

New Construction and Real Estate:

This will easily be recognized as one of the leading indicators of the country's progress. The building industry represents an annual outlay of over $6,000,000,000! Consider residential building, for example: about 200,000 residences are needed annually. The home is the first unit of society and is a foundation stone in the welfare of the people. Hence, construction of dwelling houses and accompanying real estate operations are of vital importance. When business is booming, when everybody is employed and there is plenty of money in circulation, the tendency is for families to spread out, thus creating a greater demand for homes. When business gets dull and depression overtakes us, the reverse is true; consolidation of families is the rule and a surplus of houses results.

The rental situation is closely related to this subject. The more business expands and the higher rentals go, the greater is the tendency toward the building and owning of homes by the people. This was most markedly shown during the period of high prices near the close of the European War.

Factory and similar construction involves about $700,000,000 annually and is very intimately connected with the country's mercantile progress. As civic standards are raised, municipal, state and other government building, as well as institutional projects, absorbs a vast amount of capital. Of late, there has been a studied tendency, and rightly so, to do as much as possible of this sort of construction during periods of depression in order to give employment to those who would otherwise be out of work.

Real estate operations, including certain agricultural developments, involve millions of dollars every year and form the basis of one of the greatest of the country's industries. Under the above caption may also be grouped railroad construction, highway building, and the construction of waterways. For years new railroad construction was one of the important items of activity — especially from 1850 to 1890. The great West was being developed, trunk lines pushed their way across to the Pacific Coast, and a network of railroads traversed the states in all directions.

Of late years other construction statistics have vied with railroad figures for the place of first importance, but the vast terminals and track developments are still a very large item. And, since the advent of the automobile and motor truck, highway construction has also become a very important matter. That is why the various construction projects are something which must be watched with the greatest care by the business man. Closely allied with such studies are the data on the output of the steel companies; cement, brick and lumber production; and similar statistics.

Bank Clearings and Check Transactions:

In every large city and in many smaller ones there is a clearing house where bank representatives meet daily to exchange checks drawn on one another and settle balances. Bank clearings are a useful indicator of the trend of business. Their broad significance is suggested by the annual total now amounting to over $600,000,000,000.

Records of bank clearings extend far back into the past and for years have been most carefully studied. Inasmuch as in New York City the stock and bond business is of such large volume, it is customary to study two distinct sets of clearings figures: (1) clearings *excluding* New York City; (2) total clearings of the country.

In the latter part of 1918, the Federal Reserve Board began to publish statistics of check transactions or debits to individual accounts. Whereas clearings represent merely those checks passing through the clearing house, check transactions cover all checks. In other words, a check deposited at the same bank upon which it is drawn, is not included in clearings but is included in check transactions. The clearings record is likely to be distorted by bank mergers, whereas the check transactions record is relatively unaffected by such changes.

For the reasons explained above, check transactions or debits to individual accounts have largely replaced bank clearings as an indicator of business conditions.

Every bill you pay by check is thus reported to the Federal Reserve System. As a very large volume of our business is paid for by check, you can see at once what a valuable index of business activity this record is. Of course, these figures do not show the actual quantity of goods which change hands, as the size of the checks is affected by price variations. Ordinarily, price changes do not radically affect this record, but at times, especially during a great war, commodity prices reach such abnormal levels that the variation is very marked.

During these abnormal periods, commodity and security price levels must be very carefully noted when one is studying check transactions as a barometer of business. Remember they represent the total turnover of business done by the nation, just as " gross sales " represent the total turnover of a company; and this is what the whole nation figures on — the dollar value of business turnover.

Business Failures:

Failures, both in number and amount, are a good barometer of trade conditions. By ascertaining each month the average number of concerns in business

Div. II Check Transactions

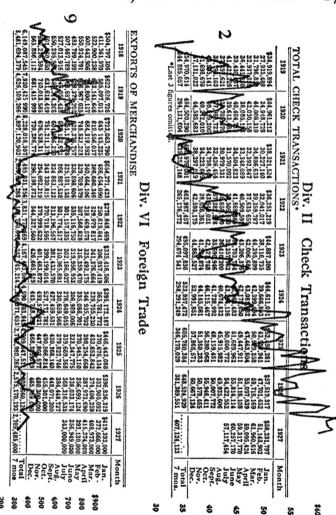

TOTAL CHECK TRANSACTIONS*

	1919	1920	1921	1922	1923	1924	1925	1926	1927	Month
	$34,919,894	$44,961,212	$38,321,524	$36,251,219	$44,887,300	$44,611,012	$57,519,317	$58,231,797	Jan.
	27,935,480	34,949,728	30,227,140	38,116,735	39,665,843	43,519,281	47,701,452	51,148,902	Feb.
	31,796,808	44,008,310	34,886,633	44,335,899	42,099,538	50,853,158	59,713,169	61,960,616	Mar.
	32,937,618	42,030,158	32,392,847	37,635,655	43,082,822	47,463,804	55,097,839	59,095,424	Apr.
	35,441,640	38,085,163	33,348,089	40,503,591	43,206,376	49,447,911	51,116,108	59,317,770	May
	39,434,607	40,484,674	34,504,823	41,703,774	42,177,250	55,814,114	55,814,114	60,257,170	June
	41,472,281	39,613,681	31,570,092	33,357,762	43,135,483	51,689,962	54,422,552	57,117,454	July
	37,197,621	41,370,774	30,979,331	35,659,130	43,136	50,600,772	49,935,606		Aug.
	41,335,111	31,518,723	32,436,454	35,398,946	41,410,200	45,915,982	49,935,606		Sept.
	41,698,670	40,391,200	34,738,674	38,138,188	40,674,832	48,159,445	55,946,411		Oct.
	37,131,022	40,545,010	43,223,649	42,871,748	41,738,992	56,280,068	50,007,772		Nov.
		44,585,683	38,355,361	41,287,874	44,145,081	51,360,283	50,578,485		Dec.
*Last 3 figures omitted.	54,970,614	483,500,250	463,987,457	495,097,836	523,957,472	609,760,384	648,524,929	Total
	44,885,057	284,131,804	265,176,372	294,674,541	338,291,249	346,178,029	381,389,551	607,124,133	7 mos.

Div. VI Foreign Trade

EXPORTS OF MERCHANDISE

	1918	1919	1920	1921	1922	1923	1924	1925	1926	1927	Month
	$504,797,306	$622,026,726	$722,063,790	$654,271,423	$278,848,469	$335,415,506	$395,172,187	$446,443,088	$419,393,000	Jan.
	361,361,970	585,097,012	685,165,225	486,454,090	250,619,841	306,957,419	361,761,787	370,676,134	372,666,000	Feb.
	522,900,238	533,141,648	819,556,037	385,680,346	329,979,817	341,376,664	339,755,230	453,652,842	408,973,000	Mar.
	500,442,906	654,319,392	840,464,106	318,469,578	316,359,470	346,935,702	398,254,668	387,973,690	415,374,000	Apr.
	550,924,791	688,967,025	745,523,223	329,709,579	307,568,828	335,088,701	370,945,110	356,699,124	391,130,000	May
	587,799,399	629,395,757	636,838,606	336,116,750	319,596,552	306,989,006	323,347,775	332,033,174	356,949,000	June
	507,467,769	618,379,200	539,757	325,181,138	302,186,027	276,649,055	339,660,368	368,316,535	343,000,000	July
	527,013,916	609,393,026	581,426,427	366,887,538	301,965,891	330,659,566	379,822,746	384,448,721		Aug.
	550,335,479	624,664,266	601,396,239	324,863,123	313,196,557	381,433,570	427,459,531	443,071,200		Sept.
	658,226,594	613,618,419	751,211,371	370,718,595	399,199,014	527,178,781	490,566,814	455,301,000		Oct.
	565,886,112	740,013,585	676,528,311	294,052,219	379,999,622	401,683,872	447,808,577	480,300,000		Nov.
		681,415,999	720,226,777	296,198,373	344,327,560	426,665,419	445,728,421	465,755,610		Dec.
	6,149,087,545	7,920,423,990	8,228,016,307	4,831,931,356	3,831,771,469	4,167,924,916	4,590,183,849	4,909,447,519		Total
	3,481,694,379	4,626,109,266	4,897,120,902	2,831,288,547	2,145,214,619	2,171,653	2,579,980,285	2,715,170,193	2,705,485,000	7 mos.

and the number that have failed, the percentage of failures may also be determined. Contrary to the ordinary impression, it is *too few* failures, rather than *too many*, that foretell disaster and panic. For instance, the records show that in 1912 and 1913 everything was running along quietly and smoothly. Nobody was scared, and failures were at a minimum, but in 1914 we ran rapidly into a crisis. The failure of the great house of Claflin & Company shocked the business world and really marked the bottom of this depression.

The same was true in the post-war period. In 1918 and 1919 people felt secure when failure liabilities were only $100,000,000 — almost the lowest on record — contrasted with a high of $700,000,-000. But how dismayed were these same unthinking people in the awful business decline of 1920 which came within a few months' time! Since then, not only have hundreds of our large business houses been wiped out, but thousands of others have been crippled and carried along under great stress by the banks. At such times inventories which appear ample dissolve to nothing when price-cutting and panic develop.

Each depression has its own peculiar type of business mortality. In 1907 large banks, especially those of New York City, went by the board; 1903 was a so-called " rich man's panic " ; 1884 was marked by many railroad failures; and some of the earlier crises were accompanied by gigantic real estate cataclysms.

After such a storm of failures the air is cleared

and the way is opened for sounder conditions. The time to be frightened is before the storm comes, when failures are very few in number.

The accompanying chart shows the close relation between failures and commodity prices. Greatest caution is required when prices are high and failures are fewest. At such times optimism rules, and only the wise ones begin to clean up doubtful accounts and prepare for trouble. The forehanded credit man can collect money and still keep his friends. But, if he waits until the storm breaks, he not only cannot make collections but loses friends as he presses for payment.

Labor Conditions:

The labor situation will be recognized at once by careful students as a vital factor in the life of the country. Approximately 40 per cent. of the total population of the United States are engaged in industry of one sort or another. Wages, unionization, strikes and similar developments are of the utmost importance. Even the increasing prevalence of machine methods does not eliminate this subject from our calculations; as the business of the country increases, the human element becomes more and more important.

There was a time when comparatively few employers knew their employees intimately. Later, the restless, selfish, money-making age resulted in employers' forgetting that labor is something more

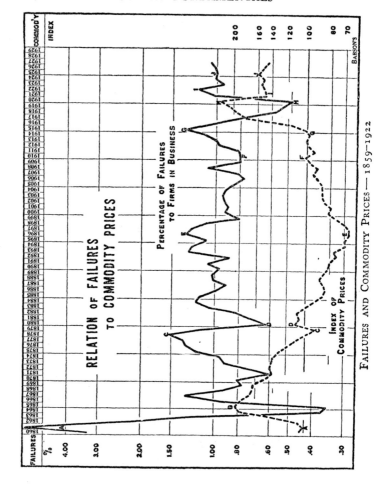

FAILURES AND COMMODITY PRICES — 1859–1922

than a " commodity." But recent years have marked the beginning of a reaction from such short-sighted philosophy.

Moreover, the standard of living is rising in civilized countries, and nowhere more than in the United States. In reality, the human relation, especially in American business, is the most critical of any. If suitable figures could be obtained, we would see it in startling relief. It is to be deplored that more data on this subject are not obtainable. One of the best sources has heretofore been a tabulation of immigration and emigration statistics. When steamers are packed with immigrants from foreign shores, this suggests excellent business conditions in the United States and high prices for labor. This, however, like everything else, can be overdone, and too large arrival figures foretell a depression. Conversely, when departures are large in number and when immigrant traffic is small, it is a good sign that United States business can get no worse. The tide generally turns upward when this condition prevails.

For years these arrivals and departures have been carefully tabulated by the Government. Prior to the World War annual immigrant arrivals averaged around 1,000,000. At times legislative influences have prevailed, tending to restrict or increase immigration in accordance with the trend of feeling throughout the country. During the World War, for instance, there were severe restrictions here, as well as drastic regulations in Europe, which practically stopped the flow of labor to this country. Later, restrictive measures were enacted for the purpose of keeping out undesirable radicals and other agitators.

The enactment of the immigration legislation of 1924 marked a new epoch in American industry. It definitely committed us to a program which was destined to have a significant effect upon labor and upon production methods. The most obvious and immediate effects of this restriction of labor supply were upon the industrial states; but any influence as fundamental as such changes in immigration laws was bound to have widespread and far-reaching reactions.

The point under consideration now, however, is that immigration statistics no longer have the same significance which they had before these restrictions were imposed. As a substitute, it would be very desirable if sufficient figures could be obtained regarding employment and wage scales for the country as a whole, and for individual localities. Already some progressive work has been done by such states as New York, Massachusetts, California, Illinois, Iowa, Maryland, Oklahoma and Wisconsin, but there is room for great extension. Of course, there are the Census of manufactures figures at two-year intervals, but in order to be of greater use to the business man such data must be more frequent. Eventually further figures from labor unions, states, municipalities, and similar sources may be available. Considerable attention is being given to the data of " Pay Rolls in Manufacturing Establishments " in the state of New York. The United States Department of Labor also issues monthly some valuable statistics on industrial payrolls.

Strike figures, if obtainable, would be an excellent indicator. The Government for a term of years kept a partial record which was very valuable, notwithstanding its meagerness. This record showed a sympathetic movement with the changes in business from a period of depression to over-expansion, and *vice versa*. Such figures are no longer being tabulated by the Government, but my organization has been for some years uniformly tabulating a certain proportion of strike statistics. Such tables will become increasingly important.

Money Conditions:

This includes banking figures, reports of the Comptroller of the Currency, money in circulation per capita, etc. Since money is used in all trade, it is one of the most sensitive indicators. All the items in the bank statement are worth watching; but the subject in which I am most interested is bank loans. It is of the highest importance to know how much business concerns and individuals are borrowing. During times of over-expansion the majority not only spend all they make, but utilize all the credit they can command. During such periods an inordinate gain in bank loans causes temporary business activity, but a decided fundamental weakness. Conversely, in times of depression, the very best sign is to see bank loans being reduced. This means that the " spree " is over and people are getting back to sanity again.

Two sources of loan statistics are readily available. One is the " loan and discount " item reported each week by the leading member banks of the Federal Reserve System, a reliable measure of the increase or decrease in the total borrowings of the whole country. The second is the report of " bills discounted " by the twelve Federal Reserve banks. When a local bank is unable to supply its customers with loans, it may re-discount certain of the notes it holds with its Federal Reserve bank. In a general way, the item, " bills discounted," indicates the extent to which the member banks have had to call upon the reserve banks for assistance.

In judging the banking situation, we must take into account the *supply* of money, or credit, which the banks have, as well as the *demand* for it. The rental price of money (interest rates), like the rent of anything else, is governed by the law of supply and demand. The supply of money is best shown by the ratio of the banks' reserves to their liabilities.

Since inauguration of the Federal Reserve System, bank reserves are held chiefly by the Federal Reserve banks. If it were not for the effect of gold imports, perhaps it would be necessary to watch only the supply of money, or reserves, in the banks. Heavy imports of gold, however, may temporarily inflate reserves without offering a safe basis for credit extension. Any increase in what is called the " reserve ratio," therefore, is always carefully analyzed by the student of fundamentals.

Foreign Trade:

The principal divisions of this subject are exports and imports of merchandise, and the balance of trade. Foreign trade statistics of any country represent the business done with the outside world. The existence of many countries now practically depends on their trade with other nations. Great Britain, for instance, is essentially a foreign trading country. The United States is in a different position: we are a younger and a growing nation, with land and resources sufficient to make us more or less self-contained. But we are beginning to emerge from this provincial attitude, and our future will be different in this respect.

The foreign trade of a country bears the same relation to the nation as a whole, as the income and expense of an individual bears to the financial condition of that individual. One who for any length of time spends more money than he receives is sure eventually to have trouble. This is the difficulty which confronts Europe. Likewise it presents a problem for America.

Our exports are to some extent a seasonal proposition. Cotton, grain, and other crop shipments to Europe every fall reach substantial proportions. Copper, iron, and other raw material exports, as well as manufactured items, also swell the total. While exports are only a small proportion of domestic activity, in boom times they do represent the top layer of our total trade, which layer is desirable for successful business.

On the other side of the ledger are goods brought into the country from foreign shores. These are known as imports. Generally speaking, no country can sell goods without buying, unless it is a great creditor nation to which the rest of the world must pay interest. There must be an interchange of goods and the up-to-date trading countries expect to import as well as export in order to keep the balance of trade properly adjusted.

Large exports during the coming years will be favorable to business only when they are equalled or exceeded by our imports. A heavy excess of exports cannot in the long run be considered a good condition. Therefore, in interpreting foreign trade statistics, it is essential that imports and exports be considered together. Strange as it may seem, an increase in imports is fundamentally a favorable sign for the future. A proportionate increase in imports and exports indicates improving business, while a decrease in both indicates decline.

Gold Movements and Money Rates:

This subject really includes gold exports and imports, domestic and foreign exchange, domestic and foreign money rates. Gold is the basis of exchange for all leading countries. It starts from the mines and is passed through its leading distribution centers to those who pay the highest price for it. After distribution, it flows from one part of the world to another, according to supply and demand.

The balance of gold imports or exports is governed primarily by our foreign trade and is an indicator of the country's credit position. Of course, gold may be artificially imported by the banks. They have even been able to postpone panics temporarily by such methods. Ordinarily, however, money, like water, seeks its own level. That is to say, if money rates are low in the United States but high in Europe, gold will gradually be shipped to the high bidders in Europe. As this movement continues, foreign rates will ease and United States money rates will strengthen. It is for such reasons that keen students continually study gold movements, money rates, and exchange.

Practically all business is carried on by a utilization of credit; borrowing for either a short or a long time is necessary. The rates for loans — money rates — vary according to the demand and supply of credit, and money rate statistics are exceedingly valuable. A period of over-expansion is generally marked by high money rates at home and in leading foreign countries, and during the progress of great wars the whole machinery on which these subjects hinge may be thrown out of gear.

During the World War extensive European purchases in the United States produced a net balance of more than $1,500,000,000 gold in this country. After the War we had more than a third of all the monetary gold in the world; while many other countries had not a sufficient supply to serve as a basis for their monetary systems. Of course, such countries must eventually return to a gold basis or completely change their monetary standards.

Commodity Prices:

There is no more interesting and possibly no more valuable subject than commodity prices. Everybody is interested in the rise and fall of prices of the articles with which we deal in everyday life. Merchants and manufacturers turn immediately to the daily papers to see the live stock, grain, metal and other commodity quotations. Commodity prices are perhaps the most sensitive barometer we have, with the exception of the security markets.

This was clearly illustrated in the precipitate decline which began in the middle of 1920, and, together with other factors, resulted in the failure of thousands of business concerns. The wholesale price index of the Department of Labor declined from the high point of 247 in May, 1920, to the low point of 140 in 1921 — a drop of 43 per cent. The Babson Commodity Index also declined with startling rapidity.

Rising prices mean increasing profits and lead to

over-expansion.   Such declines as the one just mentioned mean ruin.   As commodities go up, it is an
easy matter for the business man to buy a stock of
goods and make a profit.   He cannot help making
money.   Toward the peak of the price advance and
on the downward side he is in exactly the reverse
position, but he may always be prepared if he studies
fundamental statistics.

Not only do business men study the various combined commodity price indexes, which show the general trend, but they also give close attention to the
various groups.   All groups do not often move in
complete unison.   There are raw materials, manufactured materials, cotton, grains and other crop commodities, iron, copper, and similar groups.   Each has
a definite relation to the business trend.

Very closely related to this subject is the matter of
world gold production.   When gold is mined at the
rate of over $1,000,000 a day it is evident that these
figures must be watched to see the effect of this
supply on the inflation of prices.   This is because
gold is our measure of value.   Our whole business
system is built around a structure of values.   That
is why commodity prices, which represent these
values, must be watched with great care.   All business contracts are based on prices.   The greatest
calamities which business men have suffered have
come from misjudgment of the trend of this fundamental barometer.

Investment Statistics:

The investment markets portray the attempts of millions of people — foreign as well as domestic — to acquire what seems to them the best investments and to forecast in the most practical way the business tendencies of the country. In the most practical way, I say, because they back their judgment with their money! Thus the big exchanges of the world carry on dealings aggregating billions of dollars a day, not to mention a very heavy volume of trading in outside markets. Most buyers and sellers of securities endeavor to anticipate price changes, and leading bankers and brokers have statisticians continually studying fundamental statistics for that very purpose.

Some go so far as to say, " If I know what the New York stock market is doing, I need no other business indicator." Other merchants and manufacturers say they desire to know nothing whatever concerning stock quotations. Of course, neither view is correct, but my experience of many years proves conclusively that this subject may well be included as a business barometer. The two divisions to be tabulated are (1) price quotations, and (2) volume of transactions.

Both bond and stock prices are quoted on the New York Stock Exchange. These classes are essentially different, and statistics of both groups must be carefully kept separate. Sometimes weeks will elapse without much change in prices. At other times there

will be violent movements up or down, embracing
the whole list, or only limited sections, as the case
may be.   Day-to-day movements have practically
no value for the student of fundamentals, but the
trend over the months and years is a very good
barometer.   Short movements have little value because prices can to a certain extent be manipulated
by powerful " pools."   But no manipulator can indefinitely buck the longer trend of fundamental conditions.   In fact, such interests keep this trend carefully in mind.

Price quotations and volume of transactions
should be studied together.   The volume is very
large toward the culmination of bull movements,
and again on the down-side when liquidation is well
under way.   When the volume is smallest, prices
are low, and nobody is interested in stocks.   The wise
ones are then accumulating bargains.

As in commodities, the various groups should be
watched.   Railroad quotations were for more than
fifty years the most important section of the market,
both in bonds and stocks.   Of late years industrials
have come to the front, and during the World War
they were leaders in activity.   Coppers have always
been a leading group and public utilities often attract
general speculative interest.

In connection with investment statistics we must
not overlook such subjects as new securities, new incorporations, and re-financing.   These will be discussed later.

Crop Conditions, and Other Raw Materials:

The United States has always been extremely rich in natural resources. Its minerals, its grain, and its cotton are in demand all over the world; and over one-third its population are farmers. Hence, the great importance of this group of barometers. Vast areas in the great West are dependent for their buying power on the success or failure of agricultural pursuits, and our lives would be vastly changed if it were not for the wonderful productiveness of our rich country.

When we think that grain, cotton, iron and steel to the value of several hundred million dollars each are exported to foreign shores in a year, the importance of these subjects is evident. Many industries are absolutely dependent on the crops, and a large group of commodity prices are directly affected thereby. The railroads are particularly affected by crop conditions. The crop outlook through the growing season is followed with the greatest interest, and in this the whole country is aided by the Government, which collects the necessary data and makes very dependable forecasts at intervals throughout the growing season.

Manufactures:

Until recent years, relatively little data was available indicating manufacturing activity. Business men have always realized the importance of watching the course of manufacturing for it has had a growing effect on the purchasing power of the country both through the rapidly rising standard of living of industrial workers and the need for increasing amounts of raw and partly fabricated materials. The biggest impetus to industrial development began with the World War. Along with this, additional industrial production data became available, furnishing the business man with more tools for charting the course of business.

Some industries are so basic in their effect on business activity that every wise business man recognizes the necessity of following the trend of the statistics concerning them. Some idea of the dominating position of basic industries may be obtained from the following United States Census estimates of value for 1925:

Food and Kindred Products	$10,419,000,000
Textiles and their Products	9,123,000,000
Iron and Steel and their Products (not including machinery)	6,462,000,000
Lumber and Allied Products	3,689,000,000

Railroad and Industrial Profits:

Railroad earnings really serve as a double barometer of business. The gross earnings act as a good indicator of the general business activity. Just as check transactions represent the total volume of purchases made in the United States, so do railroad earnings indicate manufacturing and agricultural activity. Most of the goods bought must be transported by the roads. In every period of business depression gross railroad earnings decline, and when conditions improve they are among the first barometers to advance. In 1914, at the depth of the depression, gross railroad earnings were only $12,300 per mile, although some of this was due to increased rates. In 1920, they were $26,600 per mile, more than twice as large. Net railroad earnings, while very important, serve a different purpose as a barometer; they reflect more directly the financial condition of the railroads themselves.

Prices of rail securities are directly dependent upon railroad earnings — in fact, the markets discount to a certain extent these reports. As most investments are either directly or indirectly dependent on railroads, railroad earnings are of great importance to the investor. Moreover, they are one group of corporations which regularly report their earnings each month. Since only a few other corporations report so frequently, this is of great advantage to the statistician.

Because of the lack of frequent reports, it is much harder for the student to get a line on the progress of industrial projects. Yearly operating figures are generally available, but as far as monthly statistics are concerned, we are largely limited to a record of industrial dividend payments. These indicate some measure of the prosperity of the manufacturing busi-

ness of the country.   In connection with the railroads, it may be mentioned that freight car statistics
have for years been a barometer.   Idle car figures are
obtainable each week, and freight car loadings by the
various groups are often utilized.

Social and Religious Factors:

Certainly, there is a relation which holds between
politics and business conditions.   I am continually beset by people who ask me if the political outlook does
not suggest certain changes in business.   At times this
may be true, but a study of fundamentals shows that
the trend of political factors is more an effect of the
other business fundamentals than a cause.   One thing
is sure — the rotation of business seasons has often
put a political party in power or caused its overthrow.

Under this head should also be tabulated statistics
on general confidence.   I have in mind new securities issued, new incorporations, and re-financing.
When confidence is created and we are working
toward better business these figures show startling increases.   During periods of decline and depression
the reverse is true.   Such figures as above stated, however, are but a meagre measure of this most fundamental group of indicators.

A stream can rise no higher than its source; and
the prosperity of a country is absolutely dependent
upon its moral and social conditions.   Rome and the
other rich ancient nations fell when 5 per cent. of
the people held 95 per cent. of the wealth, lived in

extravagance and sin, and oppressed the other 95 per cent. of the people. It is an unanswerable argument that the statistics of new members of the nation's leading churches show great gains when the country is in a depression, and declines when the country, in the midst of a boom period, is throwing away money and burning the candle at both ends! Never forget that the progress of the country depends upon the vision of its people. " Where there is no vision the people (and business) perish."

It has been said that there never has been a panic which was not caused by disregarding either the Ten Commandments or the multiplication table, the two great fundamentals of business. I dislike unduly to emphasize this fact for fear of being thought hypocritical. Nevertheless, over twenty years of study of business conditions shows this to be absolutely true. Moreover, it is evident that the multiplication table is only a tool of the Ten Commandments.

Hence, when studying fundamental conditions, give more thought to the Ten Commandments — look first and last at the attitude and purpose of the people. When a nation is in a period in which the great majority are seeking only pleasure and doing as little work as possible, then one may easily foretell disaster and unemployment. When a change for the better has come over the nation and men are again honest and industrious, it is safe to foretell prosperity and progress.

CHAPTER III

MAKING FIGURES TALK

THERE is no sense in collecting and compiling statistics unless they are to give some valuable information about one's present relative location and the direction in which one is headed. It naturally follows that they should be reduced to a form that will give this information quickly and truthfully.

Most people are " eye-minded; " that is, the eye is quicker than the ear, if we may paraphrase the old-fashioned sleight-of-hand performer. When you read a page, it is the ear that is really working. Consciously or unconsciously, the printed letters, seen by the eye, are formed into a word which is spoken in the mind if not spoken audibly. Hearing the word, the brain connects it with an image and the subject is understood. In the case of a picture, the process is much simpler. The eye registers every detail at a glance and the image is received by the brain without any translation whatever. That is why it is quite impossible for the average person to carry six or seven figures in the mind at the same time and perceive the relative value and position of each. If they can be made into a picture, however, the same mind will read the results through the eye immediately. Incidentally, the concept will remain in the memory much longer than any explanation of the same idea through the printed word.

It is evident, therefore, that to be of value and to serve their purpose most statistics must be reduced to pictures. These charts, as we call them, were once the exclusive property of engineers, architects, and technically trained men who learned to use them in connection with plans and specifications for the presentation of more or less involved ideas to non-technical minds. Of late, however, they have come into their own in the business world. Hence, an understanding of charts is a very necessary part of one's business education. It is important to be able to understand a chart; otherwise, the greatest value of all useful statistics is largely lost. It is also vital that one be able to make simple charts to illustrate one's own ideas and to demonstrate them easily and quickly to others.

There are only half a dozen forms which can be used to illustrate almost any data or information. Since each of these has its own particular use, the results are liable to be disastrous if they are not kept in their proper place.

To begin with the simplest problem, suppose we want to make a chart illustrating the relation between the volume of business done by two competing manufacturers. Let's say, for instance, that A's sales are $200,000 and B's sales are $400,000.

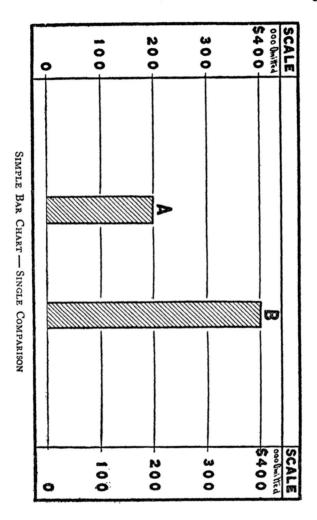

Simple Bar Chart—Single Comparison

This comparison can best be illustrated by what is known as a vertical bar chart. Simply draw a horizontal line across the paper as a base. A vertical line near the left-hand edge of the sheet will then serve as a measure or scale. In this case, you might decide that an inch represents $100,000 in sales. If this is the case, a point on the vertical line, one inch above the base line, marks $100,000; a point two inches above, $200,000; and so on. When the scale is completed, we have one point two inches above the base line and another point four inches above the base line. Let these points locate the tops of two vertical bars, about one quarter of an inch wide, which run from the base line to these levels. They may be made as wide as you like, sometimes taking the form of a rectangular block so that they can be seen more easily from a distance. The point to bear in mind is that a barred chart compares the length of the two lines and not their width. By labeling these two vertical bars A and B, you have a picture that will be quickly and easily understood by almost any one. It tells immediately that B's business is double that of A.

If it is desired to compare the volume of these two concerns for more than one year, you'll simply date your first vertical bars 1921, for instance, and by moving over to the right on the same chart, you can make another pair of bars in exactly the same manner, which will tell the story for 1922. You now have a picture which not only compares the two concerns for a given year, but each of them with its own previous year, and also their relative position for both years. If you are going to chart several years and want to get the picture into a relatively small space for easy and quick comparison, you may make the bars for each year very close together and distinguish them by filling one in solid black and leaving the other open, or by shading it with cross lines or dots or some other distinguishing feature. Every chart, by the way, should carry an explanation which indicates clearly what each of these bars represents.

If one wishes to go a step further and show, for instance, what portion of these goods were sold at retail and what portion at wholesale, the vertical bar representing A's total business for the given year might be divided into two parts — a lower part which might be filled in solid black, and an upper part which might be shaded or left open, one part representing retail, the other wholesale trade. The total volume would still be just the same as compared with B's, but the picture would give one additional fact.

Wherever it is desirable to compare two volumes or express a single relationship between two facts, it is best to use either the vertical bar or the horizontal bar chart. The latter is exactly the same as the former, excepting that the base line is a vertical line at the left-hand side of the page.

This horizontal chart is ordinarily used when de-

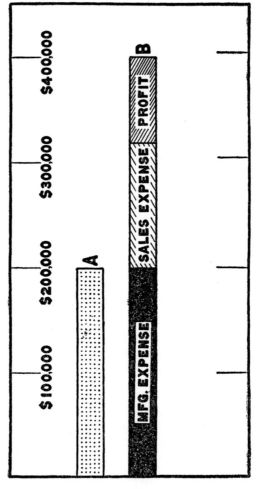

SIMPLE BAR CHART DIVIDED TO SHOW PROPORTION

siring to split the whole into several parts. If we have analyzed the sales, for instance, and want to picture the total and show what part of the $400,-000 represents cost of raw material, manufacturing expense, sales expense, etc., we construct a horizontal bar and divide it into portions which represent the various factors. For instance, if the bar is four inches long and the cost of the manufactured goods represents 50 per cent. of the total selling price, we divide the bar into halves and the two inches to the left are filled in black and labeled "Manufacturing Expense." If the sales expense amounts to 30 per cent. and the profits 20 per cent., we divide the remaining portion of the bar into fifths. Three fifths are shaded in one way and are labeled "Sales Expense," and the remaining two fifths represent the profit. This method of presentation will make percentages and fractions immediately intelligible to almost any one. No multiplication, division, subtraction or addition is necessary to see just what portion of the total is represented by each factor.

The so-called "pie chart," or circle divided into sectors, is very often used to illustrate this division or breaking up of a whole into a number of parts. While more common than the bar chart, it is not ordinarily so good, because it is more difficult to divide the circle into segments that will represent the fractions to be pictured. For this same reason it is also subject to a possible misinterpretation, because it is rather difficult to compare various areas and be sure of judging them correctly. If in a hurry, don't try to make a pie chart. You can make a bar chart in about one-fifth the time. If you do want to use the circle for purely decorative purposes, it is best to add the percentages or fractions to the chart. Write them in on the various

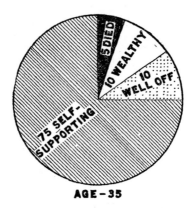

AGE - 35

AGE 35, 10 WEALTHY, 10 WELL OFF, 75 SELF-SUPPORTING,
5 HAVE DIED

pieces of the pie, so that the reader has a check on his first impression.

Another form of charting that has been used for decorative effect more than anything else consists of various sized pictures of the thing that the figures represent. For instance, in comparing the sizes of armies, it is often the practice to draw pictures of soldiers of various sizes. A big soldier represents the biggest army and a little soldier represents the

smallest army. Big barrels of flour represent a
large crop, while smaller barrels of flour represent
a smaller crop. This method, of course, has the
distinct advantage of picturing the thing represented;
so that a reader need hardly bother with the explanation. One difficulty is that these same pictures
are likely to misrepresent: For example, consider
two armies, one twice as large as the other. They
may be represented by pictures of two soldiers, one
twice as tall as the other; then the taller soldier is
about four times the area of the shorter. Or if one
soldier has twice the area, his height will be about
one-fourth that of the other. In other words, there
is confusion between height and area, and this
objection applies to most picture charts.

This difficulty in presenting picture charts can be
overcome by using equal units; instead of making two
soldiers, make two rows of small figures in uniform.
The first with ten men, for instance, all the same size,
may represent the larger army; the second, with five
men, the same size as the first, may represent the
smaller army. You still have the figure of the soldier,
and there is no possible chance for making a mistake
in reading the charts, for it is seen at a glance that
the first army is twice the size of the second.

These three forms of charts will enable one to
picture any given situation clearly and truthfully;
so that the facts will be readily grasped and a clear
impression will remain. If, however, we wish to go
beyond the present or given situation and find out

which way we are headed and where we are going, it is necessary to change our form and employ the line graph.

If we want to compare the volume of sales over a period of years with the cost over the same years, we start by laying out the base line and the vertical scale exactly as we would for a bar chart. It is customary to measure off the years on the base or horizontal line and the variable factors of volume on the vertical line. We then locate our points for total sales and cost for each year, exactly as we would if we were making up a bar chart, but instead of drawing the bars from the base line to these points, we simply connect all the points representing sales with a single line. If the bars had been drawn in, this line would connect the tops of them. The line for cost is determined in the same way by drawing a line from the left-hand side of the sheet to the first cost point, then to the next cost point, then to the third, and so on. When we have finished, we have two wiggly lines which show the direction that sales and cost took each year and which also show whether cost and sales were going up at the same time or whether one was practically stationary while the other was increasing or decreasing.

If the lines run close together, or cross each other, at any point in the chart, it is advisable to make one a solid line and the other a broken or dashed line or in some way to distinguish it. Colors are very effective if they can be used without inconvenience.

In this case, a blue line might represent the total sales and a red line costs. Such distinguishing marks make it much easier to follow the lines on a chart. Almost any number of the latest factors can be pictured on the same chart if each is distinguished clearly from the others.

It is very important, however, that you bear clearly in mind that this form of chart is a line chart, that it gives present location and volume. It tells whether the factor pictured is increasing or decreasing, but it does not show the rate of increase or decrease. This last point will be clear when you see the difference between the chart just described and what is known as the ratio chart.

In the ratio or percentage chart, the horizontal scale — the years — is determined exactly as in the bar chart and the line chart. The vertical scale, however, is quite different. Instead of being composed of equal units representing an equal given increase in volume, it is arranged so that equal units represent equal increases in percentage. In the line chart we scaled one inch representing $100,000, two inches representing $200,000, three inches representing $300,000, and four inches representing $400,000. A ratio chart is arranged so that these equal distances represent an increase of 100 per cent. On the ratio chart, the first point on the vertical scale would represent $100,000. The inch from there to the next point represents 100 per cent. increase; so our second point is $200,000. The next

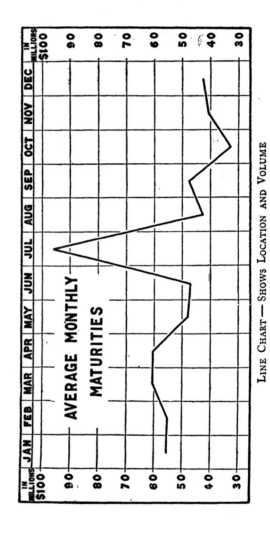

LINE CHART — SHOWS LOCATION AND VOLUME

inch represents 100 per cent. increase; so our next point is $400,000, instead of $300,000. The fourth inch doubles it once more and is $800,000. The fifth inch should be labeled $1,600,000 and so on. Once the scale is determined, the charting is done exactly as on the line chart. You can get ratio or logarithmic charting paper which makes it quite as easy to chart this way as the older way.

The ratio chart has a further advantage in that two unrelated factors about the same business, or about different businesses, for that matter, can be charted on the same piece of paper. You can chart the sales in dollars as shown on the left-hand scale that we just laid out. You can also lay out an entirely different scale of, let us say, number of employees, down the right-hand side of the sheet. You can then chart the sales and the number of employees on the same piece of paper and can compare them directly, *because both have been reduced to the common factor of percentage of increase or decrease.* Assuming that sales are plotted in the upper part of the chart and the number of employees in the lower part, when the two lines approach one another, it means that your sales per employee are decreasing. Whenever they get farther apart, it means that sales per employee are increasing.

The big thing to remember is that if you want to show the rate of growth or percentage of increase or decrease, you must use the ratio chart instead of the line chart.

The last form of chart to consider for ordinary commercial use is the colored map in which a given territory is divided into various sections, colored or

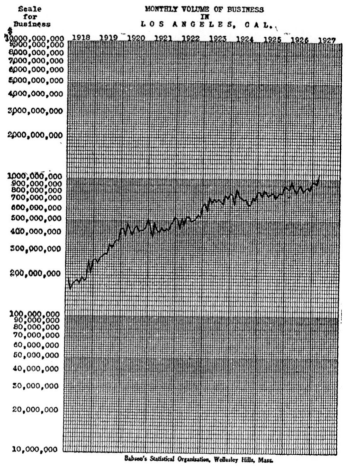

RATIO OR LOGARITHMIC CHART

shaded to represent conditions for direct comparison with other sections shown on the same map. This form is very efficient when the problem involves a given section of the country, and it can be used with great effect to record conditions of the sales field.

You now have a method of charting for almost any conceivable set of data. As we continue our study of the fundamentals, we will use several charts in order that you may become thoroughly familiar with them. You will find that they will be of tremendous help, both in your own study, and in your effort to communicate your ideas to others. Make a picture wherever possible; it is interesting and much more effective than a lengthy explanation.

FORECASTING BUSINESS CONDITIONS

FOR many years men scouted the existence of definite trends in business. There were several reasons. One was because statistical records had never been sufficiently developed to illustrate accurately the movements. The chief difficulty, however, was that no satisfactory explanation of the cause of business trends had been found. Exhaustive inquiries were conducted into the causes of panics and depressions which created such disaster.

Little progress was made, however, until the people began to realize that *the seed of panics is sown during the periods of over-expansion which precede them.*

Panics and depressions are merely the *reaction* from over-expansion, extravagance, and other excesses which develop during the times of so-called prosperity.

This discovery opened up an entirely new line of thought. It was nothing but the application to business of Sir Isaac Newton's law of action and reaction. This is one of the most fundamental laws of the universe, underlying all the sciences, from astronomy to zoölogy. This law is the basis of the steam engine, the electric dynamo, water-power installation, and every other power machine. All calculation of forces and all formulas applying to them are related to this law of action and reaction.

If there is one thing that science teaches, it is that this law of action and reaction cannot be eliminated. We may dread it and attempt to ignore it, but it is always in operation in thousands of diversified ways. Whether making a balloon ascension or raising our feet in walking, we are working in accordance with the law of action and reaction.

The study of hygiene is comparatively in the same stage in which that of mechanics was a couple of centuries ago. As a matter of history, only in recent years have fundamental laws been scientifically applied to the study of the human body. Instead of grasping the fact that the same laws apply to men as to commodities, physicians used to doctor with different methods and various drugs, hoping to hit something that would perform a cure. With the knowledge that men are simply machines there has come a great change, and doctors have learned that to do good work they themselves must be good mechanics.

Physicians now recognize Newton's law of action and reaction in its relation to sleep, breathing, eating, exercise, etc. For instance, every man has a certain normal line of sleep; that is, he requires a certain amount of sleep, which varies with different individuals at different ages, but which for a given individual at a given age, is a constant factor. As a man departs from this normal line of required sleep in one direction he must compensate by varying a corresponding amount the other side of the line. Whenever a man performs an abnormal amount of labor, causing him to lose sleep, it then becomes necessary for him to rest and make up a corresponding amount. If he attempts to ignore the law of action and reaction and continues his excesses, he becomes ill, and is forced to go to bed and make up his required amount of rest. This law of action and reaction applies in the same way to man's breathing, eating, and exercising.

Not only are certain physicians making progress to-day through the use of Newton's law, but psychologists as well are employing it in their experiments. It is a fact well known to students of Newton's investigations that the great scientist found this law to apply, not only to mechanical and astronomical phenomena, but also to affairs more remotely removed from such sciences. The student of McLaurin's famous treatise, " Sir Isaac Newton's Philosophical Discoveries," will find that Newton believed that the voluntary actions of men *en masse* are subject to the law of action and reaction.

By applying Newton's law, many of the various business subjects which I have previously described as fundamentals become *barometers* of business, instead of mere *thermometers*. Take, for example, the subject of business failures. When reports show a small number of failures, it is said that the credit situation is very favorable. Viewed in this way, failures are only a thermometer of business. Applying the law of action and reaction, we know that an unusually small number of failures means that the ordinary process of " weeding out the weaklings " is not taking place and that later the number of failures will run as high above the average line as they previously were below. Used in this way, the failure statistics become a *barometer* of business and are invaluable to the business executive in planning his policy of credit extension.

Likewise, an excessively large volume of check transactions indicates exceptional activity at the time. If one used them as a thermometer, he would feel justified in building a new factory and in laying in heavy stocks of merchandise. Applying Newton's law, the executive knows that excessive activity indicates that business is near the peak of the expansion. Instead of extending his plant, he builds up a good balance of ready cash in the bank, reduces his stock of materials, and prepares for the break which must follow.

In the same way each of these business subjects has its own significance. While no one subject can be relied upon at all times, the majority are always more reliable. The best plan, therefore, is to combine a number of basic subjects, representing the more important phases of business activity, into a single index the same as you would combine the prices of a group of commodities to form a commodity price

index.   It is well to correct the original figures in
order to eliminate the effect of seasonal fluctuations.
Such a combination of subjects gives a graphic picture of the net effect of all upon business activity.
The Babsonchart is just such a graphic measure of
business.

The Babsonchart. — The Babsonchart described is
based on 45 different subjects, carefully weighted,
and carried back over a twenty-three year period.
In addition to its use as a measure of general business
it can be broken down into four component groups —
Production of Basic Materials, Agricultural Market-
ings, Manufacturing and Distribution.   This Babsonchart represents the physical volume of business
as measured by quantitative data.   The subjects included are given in the Explanation of the Babsonchart at the right of the chart.

The line X–Y represents the country's net gain
or growth.   Based on the economic theory that action
and reaction are equal when the two factors of
time and intensity are multiplied to form an area,
the sums of the areas above and below said line
X–Y must, over sufficiently long periods of time,
be equal, provided enough subjects are included,
properly weighted and combined.

The net growth of business is something to which
every business man should give careful attention,
though economists and statisticians always disagree
as to the proper location of such a trend line.   This
one is located by the method of Moments, for the

periods 1904–1915, and for 1915–1926, connected by a line similarly computed for 1914 and 1915. Up to the beginning of the war in Europe, the long-time growth of American business continued at a fairly steady pace. From 1914 to the time the United States entered the war, there was an entirely new situation — a tremendous demand for American goods without corresponding foreign competition. Prices rose to high levels, stimulating the greatest development in that length of time that American producing facilities have ever known. After the United States entered the war the advantage was reduced. Production, already high, was expanded at a less rapid pace. The X-Y line herewith presented is in keeping with these facts.

The high levels of the stock market have tended to come in the earlier part of the over-expansion areas, and the low levels have tended to come in the earlier part of the depression areas; although in 1914 the war held prices of both stocks and bonds down longer than usual. Low money rates and high bond prices have usually come near the end of the depression areas, and high money rates and low bond prices near the end of the over-expansion areas.

Here we have a picture of American business from 1904 until the present time. It shows exactly where we are and where we are going. It tells when to buy and when to sell. The alternate areas of over-expansion and depression are evident. And, since each of these consists of a well-defined succession of steps, one can, by following this chart, forecast coming conditions in almost every field of business activity with remarkable accuracy.

Let us trace the various steps in a typical swing from over-expansion to depression and then back again. Beginning with a period of prosperity, we have usually had high money rates and real estate prices. As prosperity increases wages mount and producing costs rise. Too much money leads to dissipation and inefficiency, which are reflected in every one from the president of the business to the chap who sweeps out the shops at night. Inefficiency and increase in costs naturally force prices up, and when commodity prices rise interest rates go with them and bond prices go down.

Inefficiency then develops into downright dishonesty. Business becomes demoralized. The decline is under way, public confidence disappears, pessimism is the vogue, and stock prices tumble. As dishonesty becomes more general there follow the cancellation of contracts, petty thefts and sabotage. Increased unemployment naturally aggravates this, and the crime wave follows.

When public confidence is shaken the purse strings tighten, business falls off, and forced sales break prices. Once they are on the toboggan, commodities drop almost overnight. Finally, business is thoroughly disorganized and hard times are upon us in earnest. Ambition and initiative have been discouraged by a series of reverses; many business men are flat on their backs, figuratively speaking, and are making no effort to get up. Shops and factories are closed. Bread lines are in evidence. The political party in power is doomed for defeat at the next election.

As unemployment continues we experience a phenomenon best described as the consolidation of homes. The young folks who branched out for themselves and set up their own establishments during the period of over-expansion now move back and " double-up " with their parents to save rent. This naturally reduces the number of dwellings occupied and cuts down tremendously the demand for improved real estate, and declining real estate prices follow.

About this time those who are lucky enough to have jobs appreciate them and go to work with a vengeance. Recent reverses have taught a lesson, and thrift takes the place of extravagance. Now, just as soon as 51 per cent. of the people begin to produce more than they consume, we build up a reserve power and fundamental conditions begin to reflect improvement. Increased activity means that a man does more work for a day's pay than he did during the rush times. Wages in many cases have been reduced. The two combine for a lower labor cost. The manufacturer is then able to reduce his prices to the legitimate consumer and on the new basis can get a certain amount of business. Because consumption of goods has been cut down and money is being saved we rapidly build up a surplus which forms the basis for a period of improvement.

We here begin to see a justification for the old adage, " We take our troubles to the Lord, but run to the Devil with our happiness." The dishonesty of the period of decline has given way to a quickened religious interest. Hard work is good for every one's soul, and most persons are too busy holding their jobs to get into much trouble.

As stocks go down, we find that the dollar will buy more. Lack of activity lessens the demand for money and interest rates decline automatically. Bond prices rise. The student of fundamentals who bought bonds during the period of decline is rewarded for his foresight and courage.

As industry and thrift continue, the signs of improvement become more evident. Stock prices strengthen materially in anticipation of the resumption of industrial profits. Again the student of fundamental conditions who bought his list of stocks when those who knew no better were pessimistic and afraid to buy is rewarded for his foresight.

As improvement progresses, prices become stabilized at their new level, and the general public begins to buy again. Business activity returns to a satisfactory basis, almost every one is employed, and prices gradually strengthen under increased demand.

During the period of prosperity, rabid speculation sets in in earnest. Profits are large, and every one is expanding. There is a great demand for money.

High interest rates result and general expansion demands more room.   Real estate prices, for residential property as well as for business sites, advance. The stock market goes on a spree of speculation. Wage workers wear silk shirts.   Every one seems to forget the lessons learned during the last period of depression.   To get something for nothing seems to be the fashion.   We begin to spend more and produce less.   Right here we prick the bubble and go down on the toboggan into another period of decline.

The possibilities for profit for the average business man and investor are evident.   He not only has an opportunity to protect himself against the changes which ordinarily wipe out over half one's profit, but by knowing coming conditions, he can lay his plans so as to profit to an amazing degree.   This will be described in detail in succeeding chapters.

Some students have always doubted the " cycle " theory of business.   If they mean by " cycle " that four years of wild boom must be followed by four years of depression, three years of depression must be followed by three years of over-expansion, etc., etc., I agree with them.   I will go even further.   I do not believe that we need to have these tremendous fluctuations at all.   We could have continuous well-being and real prosperity along the X-Y line of the country's growth if we would but be temperate and sane.

The law of Action-Reaction, however, is absolute, and as long as we insist on over-doing and over-expanding we must expect an equivalent area of re-action below the X–Y Line. So long as business continues in its present habits we shall have these wave movements, and so long as we do have them it is fatal to ignore them. Moreover, every one who studies these changes and looks ahead, does just that much toward eliminating such disastrous fluctuations.

The means for study of business movements are available in increasing number and more and more business men are using them. Various federal and state departments collect and publish valuable statis-tics. Trade groups assemble data and publish it in their journals. Various statistical bureaus and forecasting agencies are making extensive business re-search and with trained statisticians drawing valua-ble conclusions on which a business man may act prof-itably and at the same time assist in ironing out the extreme fluctuations in general business.

It is true we need more information for some lines of business but the majority of business men are either entirely dependent on their own judgment of business changes or are not properly employing the fundamental barometric data available to them. Business must be recognized as a profession and not a game of chance. If physicians diagnosed our ills as haphazardly as most business men diagnose their troubles our span of life would be quickly shortened. The span of life of most businesses is entirely too short and we fail to remember that every failure has its effect in making business unstable. If you have not the time to use all of the fundamental business information in diagnosing your own business troubles or, better yet, in preventing an unhealthy condition from arising in your business, then use the services of a business specialist. The fee charged will be ridiculously small in view of the possible business loss from failure. In fact, it is really much cheaper in the majority of cases to use the services of a specialist instead of attempting to do all of the tedious work of interpreting business data in your own office.

I do not understand how any business can safely make a budget for itself unless it has a careful diagnosis of general business conditions and its own relationship to general business movements. For instance, making a budget as we are going into a period of decline in general business is vastly different from the formulating of one at the beginning of a period of prosperity. With increasing competition more exact knowledge of one's own business and that of business in general is absolutely necessary to success.

CHAPTER V

THE SEESAW OF SUPPLY AND DEMAND

WE are now ready to apply fundamental principles to the operation of the various departments of a business, that efficiency and profit may be increased. Moreover, the successful business executive must apply such principles if he is to succeed. Competition will be extremely keen during the next few years and the advantage will be with the man who can produce quality goods at a relatively low price.

Since it will be fatal to pay too much for raw material, we may as well start with a discussion of scientific purchasing. *The law of supply and demand will put thousands of men out of business before 1940.* It will also make sizable fortunes for thousands of others who thoroughly understand its operation and take advantage of the perfectly legitimate opportunity that it affords.

In the early ages, before trading was ever practiced, families were practically self-sustaining. They built their own homes, made their own clothing, and produced their own food. As civilization progressed, the separation of interests and production of food, clothing, and materials caused specialization, which in turn necessitated the exchange of goods. At first no medium of exchange existed. For example, wheat was exchanged for cotton; lumber was exchanged for iron. This was known as barter and was practised until more convenient forms were introduced as mediums of exchange.

All sorts of products have been used as mediums of exchange. In the early days of this country, tobacco, the leading product, was used in business transactions. Wampum, a shell found on the Atlantic Coast, once served as a medium. The white shell designated a certain value, while the darker or colored shell, being more scarce, held a higher value. Later, gold and silver, due to their scarcity and natural adaptability, were gradually adopted by the leading countries of the world.

The exchange of commodities involves three basic ideas: (1) price, (2) money, (3) value. It is not necessary to discuss here these subjects in detail, but their essential meaning is important when considering the characteristics of commodity prices. In the old days of barter, if one bushel of wheat exchanged for three bushels of corn, the price per bushel of wheat was three bushels of corn, and the price per bushel of corn was one-third bushel of wheat. Today, of course, prices are quoted entirely in terms of money, which can be defined as a form of wealth generally acceptable in exchange. If one bushel of wheat exchanges for two dollars, the price of wheat is two dollars per bushel. The value of a certain quantity of goods is the quantity multiplied by the price. Thus the value of 10,000 bushels of wheat at two dollars a bushel is $20,000.

The price of an individual commodity is determined in part by the general price level of all commodities in any given period. In an era of prosperity, the general price level tends to rise. The Babson Commodity Index in the over-expansion period of early 1920 reached a peak of 224 per cent. over the base period of 1908–1912. In a period of business decline and depression the general trend of prices is inevitably downward. The commodity index figure in the depression of 1921 reached the low ebb of only 49 per cent. over the same base. There is a tendency for the prices of individual commodities to respond to changes in the general price level.

The next principle to be recognized is that the price of a commodity depends not only upon the general level of prices but also on its own supply and demand. This fundamental law expressed simply is: first, that an increase in supply in excess of the amount being consumed tends sooner or later to cause a decreasing price; second, a reduction in supply greater than that of the rate of consumption lays the foundation for an upward tendency in price. On this basis it is entirely possible theoretically to ascertain the equilibrium price level; that is, the median line that would exist when the amount of goods offered in the market equals the amount being consumed. Practically, however, in modern business an equilibrium price level cannot be maintained. A price is constantly above or below a theoretical equilibrium price line, acting in sympathy with the increasing or diminishing rate of production and consumption.

If a price trend is downward, each successive decline brings more buyers into the market, resulting in a gradually increasing rate of consumption. Ultimately the point is reached where consumption has expanded to a level that exceeds the amount being produced. Ordinarily, the price then turns upward, and during the climb, consumption, little by little, tends to diminish. Thus, the equation of supply and demand fluctuates back and forth.

It may be argued that the price of a commodity should be based upon the cost of production, but it does not necessarily follow that the cost of production always determines the selling price. The price equals either the cost plus profit, or cost minus loss. In early 1920, wool, silk, and cotton showed a marked profit, based on producing costs. Yet, by the fall of 1920, these commodities were radically under the level that represented the cost of production.

The price of an individual commodity is thus governed partly by the general level of all prices and partly by the equation of its own supply and demand. Demand involves, first, the utility of a commodity, which when measured is the amount of money a person is willing to give for it; second, the possibility of substitution or the consumption of another commodity, cheaper and equally satisfactory; and, third, ability and willingness to buy commodities. Supply consists of the volume of output of commodities to cope with the factors involved in demand.

The great problem in business is to regulate supply to the probable demand. It is by a successful anticipation of future demand that the individual is permitted to build a permanently safe industrial or commercial structure. In the normal course of events, there are three problems that must be solved, at least with moderate accuracy, to insure a fair profit. First, the prospective demand six months, a year, or two years hence; second, the probable supply during the same period; and, third, the logical cost of production and selling price justified by the changes in supply and demand. Demand, like the flow of a river, is not standardized. Sometimes it is high; again, it is low. It varies according to fundamental conditions and fluctuations in prices. High prices encourage curtailed demand; low prices stimulate increased demand. For example, during the war period, 1914–1918, consumption was maintained at a greater pace than production. Consequently, prices were constantly rising; but by early 1920 the rate of commodity production exceeded the rate of absorption, and prices could then turn only one way — downward.

Human nature also enters into the question of demand. When prices rise people often rush to

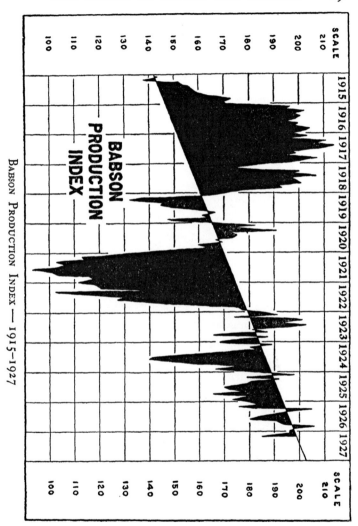

Babson Production Index — 1915–1927

market to protect future needs before a further price advance occurs. A hysterical buying movement is brought about in this manner — it becomes a sellers' market. When the tendency is downward and buyers assume an indifferent attitude, negotiating only as stock is needed — it's a buyers' market.

Supply, like demand, is an unknown factor. If prices rise, certain buying policies immediately become effective. Some build up heavy inventories with the idea of liquidating at a higher price level; others buy sparingly in anticipation of a decline. It is such factors as these that increase the uncertainty of the supply and demand volume. In addition, elements such as producing capacity, transportation, labor, strikes, and floods, are factors that directly affect supply and demand. All of the uncertainty in buying and selling cannot be overcome, yet there is a definite procedure that every merchant and manufacturer can follow which in the long run will net the highest average profit possible.

It has been already pointed out that business does not run a smooth course. The volume and value of business inevitably move in phases. As far back as the records of Babson's Statistical Organization are available — even before the Civil War — we note the four periods in business: (1) over-expansion, (2) decline, (3) depression, and (4) improvement. These movements have constantly materialized since the advent of trading. We are today in one of these stages. As time goes on we shall step to a new era, but that period and time will be followed by another fundamental change.

The same fundamental principle, namely: that underlying conditions govern the trend of business, is also true of commodity prices. One business barometer, such as crops, bank clearings, or international trade, cannot be taken as a criterion for the commodity market as a whole. Commodities must be directly associated with the composite trend of business as represented by the Babsonchart or grouped barometers.

The first step in a scientific analysis of a commodity is to determine where we are in the economic trend of business. Our position must be either in the beginning, the middle, or at the end of a period of prosperity, decline, depression, or improvement. This being found, an adequate foundation exists on which succeeding forms of analysis can be constructed. This is the one fundamental feature that the business man has long overlooked.

While individual barometers cannot be taken as a criterion, all are important as they directly or indirectly affect the commodity market. In a later chapter the relationship of individual barometers to business conditions is outlined in detail. *A reaction in the trend of an individual barometer is a warning that definite changes are not far distant.*

In the main, all barometers are important. Yet, the principal individual barometers which should be watched with constant care in connection with commodities, are failures, labor, foreign trade, production and consumption figures, transportation conditions, crops, and the money market. In relation to commodities, barometers must be considered individually as well as collectively.

Commodities are divided into two definite groups: one, agricultural; the other, industrial. The price of agricultural commodities under normal conditions responds to two elements, seasonal and fundamental. This group is dependent chiefly upon fluctuations in supply, primarily because the output of agricultural products after a certain stage is not governed by human efforts. A certain acreage is planted, so much is abandoned, and the yield per acre and the final output depend almost entirely upon seasonal developments. At the end of the season a certain amount has been produced. This may be large or small, but one point is certain, namely: the volume cannot be increased or decreased until another season. Therefore, the average price trend for the season depends largely upon fluctuations in supply. Agricultural products also adhere to seasonal tendencies, usually reaching the low point during the early part of the crop season when market receipts are heaviest. While these characteristics prevail, fundamental conditions are really the governing factor, for crop prices in addition inevitably follow the long swings of business.

The price of industrial commodities depends largely upon fluctuations in demand. Industrial production, unlike agricultural production, can be increased or decreased at will. If the price of lumber, steel, or copper advances to a profitable level, production is usually stimulated, particularly by higher cost producers. Industrial commodities as a whole do not respond to seasonal tendencies but follow in close relationship to the trend of business over a period of years. Commodity prices are seldom stabilized unless by Government intervention. Prices are constantly responding to seasonal tendencies, war conditions, panics, and major fundamental changes in conjunction with business.

A survey of commodity prices over an extensive period indicates two important characteristics. From 1900 to 1922 this country has experienced five periods of over-expansion and five periods of depression. The periods of prosperous times materialized in 1901, 1906, 1910, 1912, and 1916 to early 1920. The periods of depression covered 1904, 1908, 1911, 1914, and 1920. It is interesting to compare the trend of prices with the trend of business during the five periods completed since the first of this century. Five complete commodity price phases stand out prominently in sympathy with the business trend. The economic price pendulum is constantly swinging and will ever accompany the trend of business upward and downward. These major price trends cover a period as limited as three years, while during an era of artificial conditions such as materialized from 1915 to 1920, the time limit extended to seven years. It should be borne in mind that during the upward and downward movements, commodity prices do not run a smooth course. Irregularity and substantial reactions are constantly developing, reflecting current conditions.

The movements of three to seven years supplement a longer phase which covers a period of twenty-five to thirty years. Since the American Revolution three of these phases have materialized. The low points were reached in 1783, 1848, 1898, and the peaks in 1809, 1865, 1920. The accompanying chart illustrates this tendency. It is interesting to note that the Napoleonic, Civil, and World Wars mark the high points in the longer phases, and that the lows, in the first two cases, were not reached until twenty to thirty years later.

From the foregoing it is evident that commodity prices have characteristic trends. Prices have been considered in composite form as represented by the leading indexes, but this does not mean that commodity prices constantly bear the same price relationship to each other; all commodities do not turn upward or downward in price simultaneously. Each commodity, whether it is iron, steel, butter, or wheat, covers its own individual price trend. It is practically impossible to find in any stage of business a perfect alignment of prices. Some are high and others low. The individual commodity trend moves ahead of business, in harmony with business, or follows a retarded tendency. Moreover, these trends are constantly changing. In one period a certain group

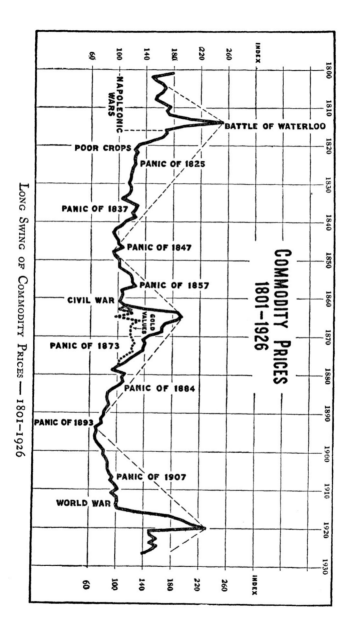

Long Swing of Commodity Prices — 1801–1926

may precipitate the price movement, while again it may assume an inactive attitude.

Briefly, we have found (1) that agricultural products are dependent on output, following distinct seasonal tendencies, also adhering to the underlying long-swing trend of business; (2) that industrial prices tend to ignore seasonal tendencies, reacting in sympathy with the volume of business; (3) that commodity prices follow developments of three to seven years' duration; (4) that there are longer phases covering a period of twenty-five to thirty-five years; and (5) that each commodity has an individual trend.

Thus far the first three steps of commodity analysis have been mentioned. First, the location of business by a composite of business barometers; second, an analysis of individual barometers; and third, an analysis of price. Now the statistical position must be considered. The statistical field that follows a commodity step by step from the mine, forest, or field, to the finished product is tremendous, sometimes involving as many as thirty to forty separate phases. This compiling appears to be an enormous task, yet it is entirely possible in this business era to obtain authentic statistical facts on the important commodities in the world.

As an illustration, take the agricultural product, wheat. First, we must know the United States acreage year after year, the yield per acre and the production derived. Next we consider the average

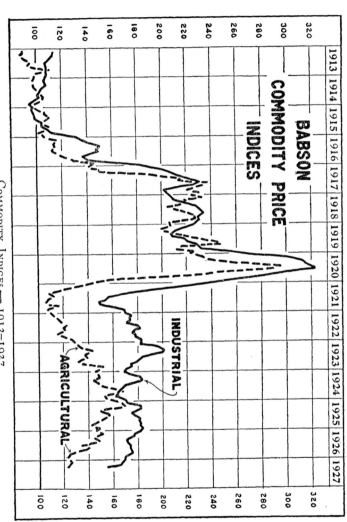

COMMODITY INDICES — 1913–1927

price to the producer, the total farm value, and the average price at the primary markets of distribution. Then there is the question of stocks, it being possible to follow the increasing or diminishing tendency monthly, in conjunction with the rate of consumption. It is then necessary to cover the volume of imports and exports and the carryover at the end of the crop year. Following this the addition of world conditions, covering production, consumption, and stocks, provides a complete statistical arrangement for any one interested in those factors that directly or indirectly affect the price.

The eleven principal features that make up an industrial analysis are as follows:

(1) Production — domestic
(2) Production — foreign
  (a) monthly
  (b) yearly
(3) Consumption, domestic
(4) Consumption, foreign
(5) Stocks on hand, domestic
  (a) warehouses
  (b) mills
  (c) storage
(6) Stocks on hand, foreign
(7) Market movements
  (a) shipments
  (b) deliveries
(8) Visible supply
(9) Imports
(10) Exports
(11) Price

It is not always possible to obtain comprehensive figures over a period of years covering all of the eleven different phases mentioned. Yet it is extremely important in any analysis for the purpose of determining future price changes, to take into consideration at least four principal items, namely: world production, the rate of domestic output, volume of foreign trade, and the conditions existing in the principal consuming outlets. However, the most successful policy calls for the adoption of a scientific method which automatically takes into consideration all factors that are bound to influence the future status of the price trend. Such a system is found in the Babson method of analyzing commodities.

A word regarding its application should be of interest. In September, 1924, this statement appeared in Babson's Reports: —

"*Unbalanced Conditions Feature Oil.* Late statistics show that there has been no fundamental change in the position of petroleum. Total output for the first eight months approached 474,659,000 barrels, against a previous five-year average for the first eight months of the year of 338,-186,000. The important point, however, is that August represents the third consecutive month in which production has dropped materially under the total of last year. The rate of flow into consuming channels has been affected by weather and adverse business conditions and since the middle of the year has failed to equal last year's volume.

The net result of output and imports, minus consumption and exports, was an uninterrupted climb in stocks. The estimated figure on September 1, is close to 360,000,000 barrels. A normal yearly increase in stocks is necessary, but the current figure stands 75 per cent. over the previous September 1 five-year average. These figures show conclusively the basis for the material price readjustment of the past five months. Until production drops or consumption expands to a point where there is a better balance, there is little justification for an advancing price trend. Meanwhile, prices have discounted much of the unbalanced condition. Mid-Continent oil is now only fractionally above the extreme lows of late 1923 and 1921. A further broad decline is not indicated. Certainly this period demands careful watching. Clients should be in a position to make some contracts on further declines.

Fuel oil prices have responded to the conditions mentioned above. In fact, the decline has been in process since the peak last February. Production has exceeded consumption for the year to date and stocks are naturally near the highest point on record — in August estimated at 46 per cent. over the previous five-year average. There are certain factors which indicate a check in the downward trend and more firmness later in the year. We refer to (1) the substantial price decline; (2) the strengthening coal situation, and (3) the probable increase in business activity this fall. Some contracts for fall and winter warranted."

At that time petroleum was selling at $1.05 a barrel and dropped to 90 cents in October, holding there until January. Fuel oil was quoted at 90 cents in September and climbed to $1.37½ in February, 1925.

In November, 1924, the following reference was made to the petroleum situation: —

" Petroleum — Statistics show that the average production of petroleum is tending steadily downward. The same is true of the number of producing oil wells completed. This is the natural result of the sharp price readjustment. The petroleum industry is now in the process of building a better foundation and bringing supply and demand closer together. Stocks are still heavy, nearly 80 per cent. over the previous five-year average. On a comparative basis, prices are low and no further marked decline is indicated. As pointed out in our October issue, this is a period when clients should make contracts."

The outstanding question naturally is, what was the scientific method of analysis covering fundamental commodity statistics that justified this conclusion? Note the application of the previously discussed method:

(1) Babsonchart or grouped fundamentals. The Babsonchart in the fall of 1924 showed business well below normal, showing conclusively that the period of post-war inflation had been entirely corrected. Production, manufacture, and distribution were all below normal and yet fundamental conditions were sound and suggested that a period of improvement was due. The confused political situation was straightening itself out and a study of fundamental conditions pointed to a rising trend of business in conjunction with the infallible law of action and reaction.

(2) A study of individual barometers which directly and indirectly affect commodities. These, too, showed that not only was the trend of business about to turn upward, but individual barometers were

favorable to rising oil prices, which were the lowest since 1916. Labor was adequate, money rates and credit conditions favorable, while rising prices on the stock exchange pointed to an improved state of general business. Transportation was efficient and inventories were reduced. The outlook for building was favorable, in fact practically all individual barometers favored the bull side of the question by a marked margin.

(3) A study of price relationship. Crude oil prices were unusually low. There had been a decline from a level of $1.75 a barrel earlier in the year to 90 cents. Compared with commodity prices as a whole there was a fairly sound relationship. Further, a study of prices of competing fuels showed that oil prices were low enough to encourage consumption. Low prices were curtailing output and stocks would not continue to increase.

(4) A study of the statistical position from initial production to ultimate consumption. A resumé indicated that production was being reduced, while consumption was growing. Stocks had given up the previous tendency to increase and by November were declining. Automobile production and registration were increasing the demand for petroleum derivatives. Taking the whole situation, crude petroleum was working into a much stronger position.

Based on these facts, is it any wonder that petroleum rose in early 1925 to $1.57, and without setback, later rose to $1.97?

Chapter VI

SCIENTIFIC PURCHASING

HAVING the fundamental principles which govern price thoroughly in mind, we will now go about forecasting price trend which will enable us to buy our supply of material at or near the bottom of the market, and to avoid being caught with a heavy inventory when fundamental conditions indicate a market decline.

First, it is necessary to collect proper information and have it in form for convenient analysis. Hence, the use of tables of figures is very satisfactory. For example, in the case of cotton, annual figures can be taken for several decades back, covering yearly acreage, production per acre, total production, average farm price per pound, farm value, average price at primary markets, both from the standpoint of the calendar and crop years, imports and exports, world production, stocks on hand, carry-over, and consumption. Such a schedule computed on a yearly basis lays a sound foundation to determine in what direction the future price is going.

The yearly form of tabulation, however, is really the smallest part of the statistical comparison of commodities. Monthly figures are very necessary.

In this modern period of statistical information on commodities it is known at the end of each month what the volume of production, imports, or exports has been. Therefore, the entire statistical situation is revised to note the potential effect of these developments. It is possible to determine whether there is a decreasing scarcity, or a burdensome supply; whether the statistical position justifies an upward price level, or a revision to a lower plane. Price records are particularly important. It is of little value to know that the price of steel is $40 a ton, if it cannot be compared with a price in a period of prosperity or a period of depression, or even a price trend ten, twenty, or thirty years previous. A careful record of commodity prices daily, monthly, and yearly, should adequately cover the question of price.

It is difficult for the average business man to picture a true story from a mass of figures. Hence, the importance of graphic presentation of commodity prices cannot be too strongly emphasized. At a glance it can be readily ascertained whether a commodity is high or low, compared with a former period and also with a normal average. We have also found that the study of commodity prices in logarithmic chart form is helpful in the study of group commodities. Group commodities are those especially related to each other such as brick, cement, and glass, when considering building materials, or cotton, rayon, wool, and silk, when studying textiles. Under normal conditions a definite ratio exists. In a period of rapidly changing conditions the differential is usually strained. This is a warning that either one commodity has gone up too rapidly or it has not gone up in proportion with existing conditions. A growing discrepancy is a warning that a more comprehensive and careful study of the commodities involved is necessary.

It is simple enough to mention what factors and forms should be taken into consideration in commodity analysis. The chief difficulty confronting business men is to distinguish the difference between authentic sources and unreliable data. Statistical data now form an important spoke in the wheel of business. Consequently, from all sections of the globe, statistical reports and opinions are being received. All are important, for they enable the business man to feel the pulse of every market. Yet, in the final analysis, only the true, unbiased facts must be considered. Therefore, authentic sources alone should be considered. In the case of agricultural products, farm papers and periodicals, private sources, grain and agricultural associations, and Government reports from the Census Bureau, the Department of Commerce and Agriculture are at the disposal of any one interested. The facts and figures vary violently. None of the reports are 100 per cent. accurate, but it is generally recognized by the student of agricultural conditions that the most reliable and authentic statistics are received from the Government bureaus.

PRICES OF TEN STAPLE COMMODITIES

Average Wholesale Price from 1860–1926

Date	Wheat bu. Chic.	Corn bu. Chic.	Cotton lb. N. Y.	Sugar lb. N. Y.	Wool lb. Boston	Iron ton Birm.	Copper lb. N. Y.	Rubber lb. N. Y.	Pork bbl. N. Y.	Coffee lb. N. Y.
1860	$1.37	$ .73	$ .11	$.0988	$ .55	$22.70	$.2287	$ .55	$20.00	$.1306
1861	1.30	.60	.1301	.0875	.38	20.26	.2225	.55	21.00	.1275
1862	1.28	.59¾	.3129	.11⅝	.48	23.92	.2187	.48	15.34	.205
1863	1.16	.84	.6721	.14⅛	.75	35.24	.3387	.87½	18.50	.2965
1864	2.01	1.44½	1.015	$.25\frac{9}{16}$	1.00	59.22	.47	.80	44.00	.3775
1865	2.04	1.26½	.8338	.21⅝	.75	46.08	.3925	1.20	38.00	.2537½
1866	2.20	.90	.432	.16⅞	.70	46.84	.3425	1.00	34.00	.1718
1867	3.33	1.21	.3159	.15⅞	.55	44.08	.2537	.65	24.50	.16
1868	2.43	1.23	.2485	.16½	.46	39.25	.23	.67½	30.00	.115
1869	1.50	1.02¾	.2901	$.16\frac{3}{16}$	.48	40.61	.2425	.82	34.00	.0931
1870	1.30	1.02	.2398	.1351	.46	33.23	.2118	1.00	30.50	.10
1871	1.60	.77	.1695	.1312	.62	35.08	.2412	1.00	23.00	.1375
1872	1.62	.70	.2219	.1237	.72	48.94	.3556	.72½	16.00	.1631
1873	1.76	.63	.2014	.1136	.50	42.79	.28	.74	18.00	.1862
1874	1.39	.86	.1795	.1050	.53	30.19	.22	.75	24.75	.2625
1875	1.33	.84	.1546	.1061	.52	25.53	.2268	.58½	23.50	.1806
1876	1.35	.62¾	.1298	.1051	.38	22.19	.21	.64	22.75	.175
1877	1.63	.59¼	.1182	.1073	.50	18.92	.19	.58	17.95	.1943
1878	1.24	.53½	.1122	.0907	.36	17.67	.1656	.49	11.35	.1385
1879	1.24	.47	.1084	.0881	.37	21.72	.1862	.51	13.75	.1387
1880	1.30	.55	.1151	.0980	.46	28.48	.2143	.81	19.00	.15
1881	1.30	.62	.1203	.0970	.42	25.17	.1818	.76	20.00	.1212
1882	1.32	.77	.1156	.0935	.42	25.77	.1912	.87	24.75	.0975
1883	1.17	.64	.1188	.0865	.39	22 42	.165	1.07	20.15	.0931
1884	1.00	.61½	.1098	.0675	.35	19.81	.13	.96	19.50	.1062
1885	.94	.51	.1045	.0653	.32	17.90	.1083	.56	13.25	.09
1886	.88¾	.52¼	.0928	.0623	.33	18.71	.1100	.61	12.20	.095
1887	.88	.48¾	.1021	.0602	.34	20.93	.1385	.76	24.00	.1684
1888	.94	.59¼	.1003	.0718	.29	18.88	.1677	.76	16.00	.1581
1889	.91	.43¾	.1065	.0789	.35	17.76	.1349	.74	13.37½	.1765

Year										
1890	.92	.48½	.1107	.0627	.33	18.41	.156	.80	13.62½	.1793
1891	1.05	.67½	.086	.0465	.31	17.52	.1276	.78	13.00	.1671
1892	.908	.54	.0771	.0435	.28	15.75	.1156	.6763	15.05	.1430
1893	.739	.499	.0856	.0484	.24	14.52	.1075	.7167	21.80	.1723
1894	.611	.509	.0604	.0412	.20	12.66	.0952	.6744	14.57½	.1654
1895	.669	.477	.0744	.0453	.18	13.10	.1053	.7445	12.87½	.1592
1896	.781	.340	.0793	.0455	.17	12.95	.1098	.80	10.85	.1233
1897	.954	.319	.07	.0497	.21½	12.00	.1136	.8454	9.00	.0793
1898	.952	.376	.0594	.0492	.28	11.66	.1205	.9271	12.30	.0633
1899	.794	.413	.0688		.29	19.36	.1776	.9954	10.45	.0604
1900	.804	.453	.0925	.0532	.28½	19.08	.1665	.9817	16.00	.0822
1901	.803	.567	.0875	.0505	.25	15.87	.1072	.8496	16.80	.0646
1902	.836	.684	.09	.0446	.26	22.19	.1216	.7273	18.70	.0586
1903	.853	.572	.1118	.0464	.31½	19.92	.1372	.9054	18.37	.0559
1904	1.04	.51	.124	.0489	.56	12.91	.1286	1.12	14.00	.082
1905	1.01	.50	.096	.0554	.68	15.79	.1568	1.27	14.15	.082
1906	.79	.46	.1102	.0461	.69	18.37	.1023	1.26	17.33	.087
1907	.92	.53	.119	.0470	.67	23.12	.1993	1.11	17.27	.078
1908	.98	.69	.105	.0503	.50	15.60	.1339	.89	15.58	.082
1909	1.22	.67	.1206	.0487	.62	16.18	.1311	1.58	18.40	.087
1910	1.11	.58	.152	.0502	.59	15.24	.1288	2.02	23.79	.103
1911	.99	.59	.13	.0541	.49	13.68	.1255	1.21	19.15	.141
1912	1.05	.69	.115	.0524	.54	14.97	.1648	1.11	19.00	.158
1913	.99	.64	.128	.0442	.51	14.98	.1552	.91	22.08	.131
1914	1.02	.69	.111	.0502	.54	13.30	.1310	.72	22.71	.113
1915	1.30	.72	.1018	.0603	.64	13.65	.1754	.62	18.21	.094
1916	1.38	.81	.1443	.0733	.75	18.79	.2800	.73	25.96	.104
1917	2.29	1.66	.2348	.0789	1.31	40.26	.3008	.71	41.31	.10
1918	2.20	1.73	.3169	.0794	1.58	36.30	.2454	.64	48.96	.122
1919	2.23	1.67	.323	.0903	1.41	32.23	.1886	.55	51.98	.247
1920	2.32	1.43	.3381	.1652	1.30	45.17	.1786	.35	37.71	.19
1921	1.46	.58	.151	.0635	.64	27.04	.1282	.19	26.33	.104
1922	1.235	.63	.2113	.0609	1.05	24.30	.1362	.197	26.79	.142
1923	1.106	.823	.29	.0878	1.22	27.61	.1476	.276	26.20	.148
1924	1.278	.98	.29	.0765	1.218	24.11	.1328	.25	27.27	.213
1925	1.778	1.06	.24	.0568	1.209	23.84	.1425	.64	38.98	.244
1926	1.556	.767	.175	.0568	.98	24.769	.1401	.434	37.20	.223

The Bureau of Agriculture maintains records on the production and distribution of foodstuffs which run back to the development of the West. Each month this bureau issues " Weather, Crops, and Markets," which contains a wealth of information concerning production, both estimated and actual, yield per acre, weather conditions, market developments, and a diagnosis of certain commodities. During each season of the year the farmer and consumer of agricultural products are in a position to look into the future as regards the crop situation. By December harvesting returns are complete and the final figures for the year are issued.

In assimilating the industrial commodity statistics, we again have trade papers and periodicals, private sources, business associations, and the various Government bureaus. All have their place in the business field. But the most authentic information is received direct from Government bureaus and the growing industrial associations. The Government bureaus to-day have adopted the policy long practised in agricultural products. A few years ago it was difficult to determine the current rate of output of such commodities as petroleum, lumber, or cement. Now almost at the end of each month the volume of production, consumption, stocks, imports, and exports, prices, and other factors are known. The bureaus of labor, commerce, agriculture, census, interior, and the Federal Reserve System, offer a complete source for practically all information from the first stages of industrial commodity production to consumption.

We have found in our studies that each commodity follows a leading distributing center. For example, the leading hide and leather as well as wool market is Boston; sugar and coffee, New York; grain and live stock, Chicago. Therefore, it is the best policy in compiling commodity prices to cover quotations in the leading markets. There are hundreds of periodicals, each specializing in one or a group of commodities. These adequately cover the question of price and current market conditions.

The table on pages 86 and 87 shows the range of ten staple commodities, with market and average annual price, 1860 to 1927.

In most businesses, the inventories of various commodities represent a considerable investment. In times of increasing competition, such as at present, the medium and smaller sized business units especially will have to pay more attention to inventory control to insure a reasonable profit. Every business should be systematized so that production and sales schedules may be given to the purchasing agent to assist him in making his purchases.

This table of commodity prices we have just presented illustrates what opportunities there are for the purchasing agent to take advantage of the fluctuation in commodity prices. While these data are on an annual basis, the man following commodity markets should have his figures at least on a monthly basis for assisting in determining these major trends in prices. Many merchants and manufacturers have failed simply because their inventories were not carefully controlled in relation to price movements.

There are real opportunities to save money in any merchandising or manufacturing business by buying at the right time. By control of inventory money would be released for reduction of bank borrowing, for increase in surplus and dividends, and for further development of the business. A specific example of the possibility of saving through inventory control was mentioned in the preceding chapter.

To secure large profits, however, one must not make profit the great object in life. Profits, like happiness, must come through rendering service. The man who starts out deliberately to get happiness rarely finds it. Happiness is the reaction which comes from doing things for others; profits come in the same way. Very seldom does a man make even a financial success when he deliberately starts out to get rich. The great captains of industry are men who have never tried to get rich. They are men who were tremendously interested in their work, who went to it as to a game, who tried to produce or sell a better product than any one else or make the same product cheaper, and then automatically become millionaires. I am not now preaching or speaking by hearsay. Most of America's great industrial leaders, manufacturers, and merchants are known to me personally. Many of them are personal friends. I know their aims and

ambitions as well as their struggles and disappoint-
ments. They have become rich by making their aim,
not *profits* but *service.*

This fact is of great importance to the young man
in business. We hear too much about profits, price,
and pleasures; too little about service, soundness, and
sacrifices. Yet, these are the things which have made
America build cities, stretch the railroads across the
prairies, fell the forests, bridge the rivers, and develop the mines. Some of these things were done
simply for profits, but the great work was done by
men and women who cared not especially for the
profit but for the love of doing things. I am writing
this during a few days vacation at my birth place,
Gloucester, Massachusetts. As I look from my window I see boys building sand houses upon the beach.
Other boys are rolling on the sand or splashing in the
water. Is there any doubt as to which of the boys
will grow up to be the more successful men? Yet,
these boys are not making these sand houses for
profit. They simply love to construct and develop.
It is the same instinct in grown-ups that makes great
captains of industry. Profits, large salaries, and
riches come, not by seeking, but by doing. Men and
women who supply efficiently and cheaply the things
which the world needs and when the world needs
them, cannot help but prosper. But, of course, to
know what the world needs and when it needs it,
you must study fundamentals.

Chapter VII

MANAGING MEN AND ECONOMIC LAW

THERE are very few one-man businesses. In this day of specialization men find that they do one thing or one group of things better than another thing or group. The logical outcome is to hire some one who is especially adapted or who can be trained to help out in these other activities. If your business is successful it becomes necessary to hire more and more people to help carry on its various activities. Soon you are facing some very human problems in getting along with these people and in helping them to get along with one another.

This matter of managing men is one of the most important in all business. Fundamentally, it divides itself into two distinct problems. First, the management of the men with whom we have personal contact; second, the management of workers and groups with whom we have no personal acquaintance, but who are represented by a committee or union representative. The answer is the same in both cases. There is no other place in the entire fabric of the commercial world where the law of action and reaction works out any more surely than in the more or less indefinite field of human relation.

"*As in mechanics and economics, so in human relations, every action is followed by an equal reaction.*"

In the first field where the executive has personal contact the law is generally recognized. A man may not be conscious that he is employing it, but his very personal contact and experience in working with a man will lead him to apply it unconsciously. Very few initial rules are necessary in this particular field. Give a man a chance to work, give him all the responsibility that he can carry, and then let him work alone to sink or swim on his own resources. If he has the right stuff in him he will go to work with a vengeance and will develop very rapidly into an exceptionally able man. If he hasn't the right sort of material in him he never will make an executive anyway, and the sooner it is found out the better.

In the matter of compensation I have always found that it pays to give men a financial interest in their job. Wherever it is possible put a man on a basis such that he shares a part of the result of his particular work. He will work harder than it is possible for him to work on a fixed basis, and both employee and executive will make more money than they would on any other plan.

The problem of dealing with men with whom you do not come in direct contact is a much more difficult one because of the misunderstandings that are bound to arise through dealing in a roundabout way. Before I undertake the task of outlining a solution I am going to trace briefly the path of the capital-labor puzzle through a typical movement.

The attitude of labor all over the United States changes radically as we go from prosperity to depression, or *vice versa*. When jobs are many and men are scarce, labor assumes a more or less arrogant air. When we say " more or less," we mean that the greater the urgency of the labor market, the more powerful labor becomes. During the phenomenal period of the World War we saw this fact illustrated to the extreme. Never before in the history of the United States has labor had such an advantage in the market as it had during those years. Four million men were withdrawn from the productive forces of the country and put into our army and navy. Other millions were engaged in supplying these forces with sustenance and war material. The balance were left with the ordinary production work of the country on their hands. Furthermore, immigration was suspended and the ever-fresh supply of cheap labor was thus cut off.

In consequence the workers had the advantage all on their side. They were for the most part loyal and intent on serving their country. But the urgency created by mounting living costs, coupled with the power that conditions gave them, resulted in a nation-wide move on the part of labor to better its conditions.

The outstanding symptom of this development is the frequency of strikes. I give here a chart of strikes in the United States from 1915 down to the present time. All through the war and during the period of post-war prosperity, as you see, the strike curve was far out of normal. Labor was using its economic power and employers were generally unable successfully to cope with this power. The majority of the strikes were successful.

The period beginning in 1921 shows the slow penetration of Labor's mind with the fact that conditions had changed and that the tactics of the war years could no longer be followed. Labor lost its tendency to strike at the slightest provocation.

During the war period, wages on the average were doubled. In some cases, as for example in cotton textiles, they were nearly trebled. On the whole, however, they ran along about equal to the increases in the cost of living. Some of the workers did not receive increases anything like the increases in the cost of living. Others made gains in excess of such increases. During this period the attitude of the employer was generally that of practical acquiescence. True, many employers fought the increases asked for; but in the main employers realized that the advantage was on the side of labor and that all the employer could do was to limit and not block the evident tendency.

With the beginning of depression a change came. The employers realized it first. Stung by the straits

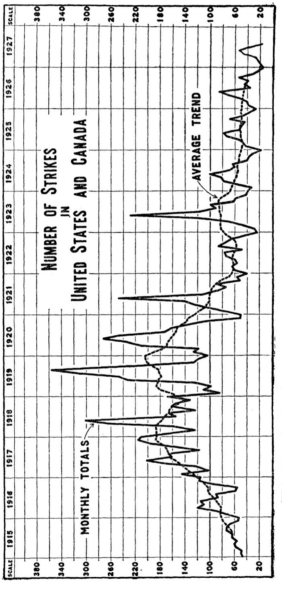

NUMBER OF STRIKES
IN
UNITED STATES AND CANADA

MONTHLY TOTALS

AVERAGE TREND

This table of strikes has been prepared from actual records collected weekly for the past thirteen years. A seasonal trend is evident, reaching its high point in the middle of the summer and the low point at the first of the year. It may have seemed to some that strikes have increased each year, but this record shows they have worked from what might be called a low point in 1915 to a high point in 1919, and have since worked back toward a low point through which they had gone during the preceding four years, they organized to get even for what they had all suffered. It is fair to say that the attitude of labor during a boom is balanced, if not over-balanced, by the attitude of the employer in years of depression. This is an exact illustration of the law of action and reaction. Labor, by its arrogance during the war, piled up for itself this reaction on the part of the employer. Or, if you wish to put it the other way, the employer, because of what he had suffered during the war, came to the front with a determination born of his experiences when labor was on top.

Labor was very slow to realize this. In 1921, when the crash began to spread over business and when men were laid off and wages began to drop, labor leaders raised a cry that all of this was a deliberate attempt on the part of employers to punish and deflate labor. An examination of the Babson-chart and a scrutiny of the list of business failures is sufficient refutation of this charge. No one suffered more than employers during that depression. Both workers and employers were caught in the swing of forces bigger than themselves. Neither was to blame; each had to suffer.

At last, however, labor in most cases realized the truth. Strikes subsided and efficiency mounted. The entire attitude of labor changed, and the employer became the master of the situation. In that position he took, very generally, an attitude comparable to that which labor assumed during the war. Now this was nothing out of the ordinary. It was bigger than anything we had ever had before, because of the artificial stimulation of the war. The swing back and forth between labor and employer is, however, what always happens as we go from over-expansion to depression, or from depression to over-expansion.

One can see this in another way by examining the history of the unions and the growth of unionization. This is brought out by the Babsonchart with the membership of the American Federation of Labor plotted against it.

Now, we undoubtedly have a set disposition on the part of labor to get together in unions of one sort or another. This desire is persistent and we may expect, therefore, to see a further growth of unionization accompanying the growth of the country and the increase in business activity.

The chart shows, however, that aside from the broad tendency toward unionization which runs through the period somewhat like the X–Y line, the membership growth of the Federation has periodically been halted or turned back. Such was the reaction which started in 1921.

These two illustrations are sufficient to show that, when we come to the relations of capital and labor, or of employers and employees, we find ourselves dealing with a vibratory movement. Back and forth the pendulum swings; from one side to the other the tide of battle ebbs and flows. It is not that either

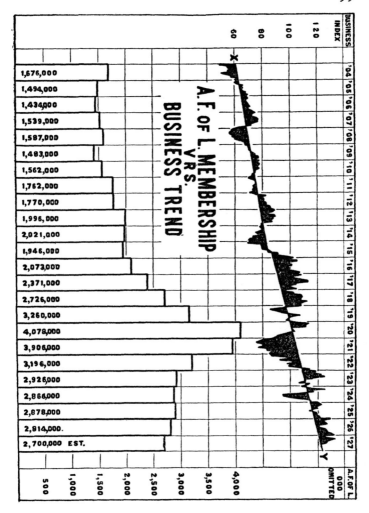

labor or capital wish it to be so. This great movement is no deliberate frame-up on either side. In fact, each side, if it could have its way, would wish to be delivered from these relentless forces which alternately deflate and inflate one another.

The real fact is that each side is caught in the mechanism of this great economic law. If they could but remember it at the right time, they might save themselves a lot of trouble. But when either side happens to find itself in possession of the ball, it plays the game as if there was nothing different coming. The great problem before each side is to learn the law, to believe in it, and to act with reference to it; so that the grind of the law may no longer bring wretchedness and suffering.

Let there be no mistake here. Employer and employee have some diverse interests. They are each buyers and sellers in a competitive market. One wants a high price; the other a cheap commodity. This separateness in interests will always exist, so long as the present social order stands. No beliefs, whether of the law of action and reaction, or of any other sort, will rid the employers and employees of the fundamental conflict which results from this diversity of interests.

On the other hand, labor and employers have so many things in common that they can learn, if they will, to work in recognition of this law, and in this way they can save themselves from much of the trouble which otherwise comes to them. For a broken law always means that the breaker, or some innocent person whom he involves with him, will suffer the penalty.

The worker must give an honest day's work. Without this an honest day's pay does not benefit him. No one can take out of a job more than he puts into it without hurting himself. This kind of action is hurting millions of workers right now. The higher cost of everything a working man buys is accounted for, in part, by the fact that he and thousands of his fellows took out of their jobs more than they put in. If every dollar of wages got a dollar of work, other things being equal, the dollar would continue to buy a dollar's worth of stuff.

The employee makes his biggest mistake when he thinks that in doing less than a day's work he is hurting the boss. Maybe he is; but he is in the long run hurting himself and every other worker more than he is hurting the boss.

It is a strange fact that this entirely wholesome doctrine seems to be better understood by the radical Amalgamated Clothing Workers than it is by the old-fashioned American working men, who make up some of the other labor bodies. Start in to have a house built, or rebuilt, if you want to see how little the average building-trade worker appreciates this fact. It has never dawned upon him that the reason he has to pay such high rent for his house is to be traced back, largely, to the fact that, when you hire him to build one for you, he does half a day's work

instead of a whole one. Such workers need to go to
Mr. Sidney Hillman, of the Amalgamated Clothing
Workers, and hear him tell his own people, that anything which injures their industry directly injures
them.

But the employees are not the only people who
need to learn the truth of the law. The employers
also need it. Perhaps they need it even more than
the employees. *The outstanding mistake of the employer is his failure to realize that he is dealing with
human material.* He must realize that the men and
women who work for him are men and women, and
that they are to be treated as such. He has intelligence to deal with, even though it is in many cases
rudimentary, and that intelligence will react to his
attitudes, just as surely as will the intelligence of his
customers and of his business associates.

The distressing thing about the law of action and
reaction, when applied to human industrial relations,
is that it is hard to chart. It is seen only as we see
its results. If the law came up and hit us in the face
every time we broke it, as does the law of gravitation,
we'd not forget it. But the penalty or reaction is so
long delayed, in many cases, that we forget the law
altogether. The result is that many of the ills which
now afflict industry on its human side are the delayed
penalties for the law breaking of men dead and gone.

This industrial relationship is no place for any
kind of charity. What ought to come about is a
realization that the relation between employer and

employee is fundamentally a business relationship. This is in consequence of the fact that we have intelligence to deal with. Just as fast as intelligence grows, comes a resentment over any hint of charity, or talking down. The more our men know, the more they demand that they be treated as men.

One thing seems to be emerging from the conflict between employer and employee, and that is labor's growing insistence on a right to a say, on equal terms, regarding the things that directly concern it in the industrial relation. The employer who does not realize this is going to run against it even more forcibly in the years right ahead. The wage worker can no longer, in the mass, be treated as a dependent or as a child. He must be treated as a man and be granted a man's right to his own say about things. More will be said about this in the next chapter. At present we wish to call attention to the fact that this is the real meaning of the trade union movement; it is labor's effort to get itself into a position where it can have its say.

Employers must recognize this tendency and grant this right. Somehow, in some way, the wage worker of to-day and tomorrow will find expression. It may be in the union; it may be in the shop committee, it may be in some other way. But somehow he is going to be consulted and to take up his duties, not because the boss says so, but because he has himself voluntarily agreed to the terms and conditions of those duties.

We have seen during the years since 1918 a large growth of the shop committee movement. There are nearly a thousand of these committees in operation in the United States. In too many cases the movement is a device on the part of the employer to get rid of the trade union. Whatever the conditions, however, the shop committee will function successfully just so far as it is an honest effort on the part of the employer to give his employees a chance to become vocal. Any employer who tries a shop committee, with the idea that he will be able thereby to put something over on his employees which he could not otherwise get past their intelligence, is doomed to be disappointed.

Shop committees which are doing the best work today are those which give the largest amount of determination to the workers. This is natural. What you put in you take out. If you sow the *expectation of responsibility*, you will get the *acceptance* of it. If, on the other hand, one uses any sort of human machinery to drug, dope, bamboozle employees, he will find that they ignore him when his back is turned and he will be quite fortunate if they are as considerate as that.

These two things, then, wait upon a realization of the working of the law: a general willingness to give a day's work for a day's pay, and a willingness to give to employees the part of men and women, rather than to regard them as cogs on the wheel. To a great degree these two go hand in hand and must come about

simultaneously. They mean a new deal in most of
our shops. It rather seems as if the first move would
have to be made by the employer. In that case much
depends on the employer's genuine conviction of the
wholesomeness of what he is trying to do and his
determination to play the game square. The man
who is not ready for this had better keep his club —
for he will have use for it.

The employer, however, who is ready to extend
honest co-operation to his employees and who is willing to go wherever that leads him, can count on
getting that back again from his employees. The law
will work. It will work anyway. What we get out
of it depends on what we put into it.

Chapter VIII

SOLVING THE PRODUCTION PROBLEM

BEYOND doubt the great problem of civilization is the problem of production. Our workmen are, on the whole, the most efficient in the world. Save possibly pre-war Germany, no nation has gone so far as we have in machine methods and quantity production. The current income of the people of the United States, according to the best figures obtainable, is about $90,000,000,000 per year, and if this income were divided equally among the population, the sum received by each person would be about $770.

The $90,000,000,000 is, however, not evenly distributed. Some few at the top get very much more than others at the bottom. In consequence, thousands farther down the line get very much less than their proportional share and fall short of the standard set for decent and efficient living.

Even if we had perfect and equal distribution — if we had Socialism or Communism or any of the "isms" that propose to make a paradise for us — we would still be confronted with the basic fact that we must have increasing production to enable individuals to meet the developing standards of civilized life. The great problem of civilization in the United States is: How shall we add to our annual production?

There are several avenues of approach to this question. One is that suggested by the report of Mr. Hoover's committee on waste in industry. This committee says that at least 50 per cent. of waste exists in even our best managed industries. The report goes on to apportion this waste among the different factors in the producing machine. A large part of the waste is frankly charged up to faults of management. The answer to the problem, according to the committee, is to give the efficiency engineer a chance to eliminate the waste that could be taken care of by improved engineering methods.

I have no fault to find with the suggestions of this report, but for our present purposes we wish to come at this problem from a different angle. There is no doubt that we are face to face with a problem more complicated than that of mere engineering. The engineers could do much for us, if they had a chance, and their remedy is *one* of the remedies that should be prescribed to meet the needs of the case. Deeper than this is the fact that we must *love to produce.*

Production has never been the basic motive of business; at most it has been but secondary. The main motive has been, not production, but profits. Our industries are not organized for production; they are organized for profit making. The wide and fundamental gap between the two is indicated in that stimulating book of the late Henry L. Gantt, published shortly after his death, entitled " Organizing for Work." If we are going to solve this problem of production, we must raise up a race of producers — we must organize industry to that end. Some new convolutions must be developed in the human brain. The ideals of life must be reformed.

If our forecasts are correct, we are starting now upon a new phase of business in the United States. The general trend of business activity was upward since 1896. Everything went up. Prices, wages, living costs — everything concerned with the maintenance of life and of business activity slowly and continuously rose for practically twenty-five years. Under such a condition appropriate laws and methods of doing business grow up. Practically all of the men who are active in business to-day have never had any experience with business under any other conditions than those of a rising market. All the rules they know by experience are the rules which fit conditions.

With the beginning of 1920 this country may have started upon what may be a twenty-five-year period to be marked by directly opposite conditions. Everything, broadly speaking, may go down. Prices, wages, costs of living — all the main factors — may be on a descending scale for a number of years.

Commodity prices have already reflected this downward tendency. Cost of living has been moving slowly downward. Meanwhile wages have not followed the downward trend, but at the present time the upward movement which has been continuing since 1920 is now definitely over. The next broad, general movement in wages will be downward.

The reasons why wages have been maintained steadily in the face of dropping price levels include (1) tremendous increase in productivity of labor through labor-saving devices and improved processes, (2) restriction of immigration which has curtailed labor supply, (3) an increased union strength of many trades, and (4) continued period of unusual prosperity.

It is fundamental to business success in the years right ahead that business men, workers — everybody — get hold of this basic change in the situation and learn to do business under it. Most of all, it is needful to keep this great fact in mind. We shall have, from time to time, as we go on, periods like the summer of 1922 when the trend of prices will seem to be upward. We must not be deceived by such transitory symptoms, which are but eddies in the main stream, while still the broad movement is the downward one to which we have referred.

Labor and labor management are fundamentally different while this condition lasts from what they have been in the experience of the men who are now managing our businesses. The main objective in labor management for the past thirty years has been to *successfully and wisely resist excessive increases in wages.* That period has gone. For the next twenty-five years the main job in labor management may be that of *successfully piloting labor through a period of falling wages.*

This is not a call for promiscuous and excessive wage cuts. The words used above have been carefully chosen. Still, it remains that the man who gets business and who makes money for the next twenty-five years will be the man who succeeds in giving unusual quality at the lowest price. The entire problem of successful merchandising revolves around that one fact. Therefore, among the foremost items of successful manufacturing is to be that of reducing labor costs, and a good part of that must come through a gradual, wise, and successful lowering of wage rates.

Labor is going to react to this fact. It is beginning to react to it now. Labor is lulling itself with the solacing thought that wages are going permanently to continue upward. Because general business has continued good the inevitable wage reductions which are ahead have been delayed. But labor is slow to realize this fact. However, that part of labor which obstinately refuses to face fundamental economics will find itself face to face with realities of the situation before very long.

This does not in any sense mean that because labor is no longer in the saddle in the period in which we are now entering that employers can consequently be ruthless in cutting wages. It simply means that as prices drop wages must drop proportionately. If this takes place in as reasonable and scientific a way as possible there will be no essential reduction in the purchasing power of the dollar. We do not mean for a moment that wages are going back to the level they were in 1913. On the other hand, the purchasing power of wages is to-day abnormally high solely because wages have not kept consistently in line with other prices.

Wherever ignorance exists the thing to do is to turn on the light. *If your employees knew as much about your problems as you do, their reaction to them would be the same as your own.* You, in your office, do what you can to inform yourself about business conditions. You read all the reports available. You receive information through your business association and, full of this knowledge, you go before your employees to ask for a reduction in wages or for some new conditions which will cheapen unit production costs. But your employees are utterly destitute of the knowledge which has brought you to your conclusions. All that they see in your proposal is reduced wages, lower standards of living, and a plan, hatched up by a hostile employer, to take advantage of them. Consequently, they resist. What seems axiomatic to you, seems to them like injustice.

If they had your background, they would feel as you feel.

The answer is: Give them the information!

We feel that this suggestion is the one big thing that we have to say to our employer clients at this time. All material such as the Babson Statistical Organization furnishes to its clients on fundamental business conditions and upon industrial problems, must be reshaped for presentation to your employees. They must be enabled to look at things through the same eyes as yourself.

For example, take the Babsonchart. It is a picture of business conditions, presenting in graphic form what you are contending with in the general business situation. Use such a chart with your employees. We base all of our business forecasts upon this chart. You should use this chart or some other to pass these things along to your employees. Have these charts copied on a large scale or put upon a lantern slide, and kept up to date. Then you, or your employment manager, must regularly and frequently explain what the charts mean to the employees. Simple language with much repetition and almost infinite patience will be required; but it will be worth while.

In similar fashion, the particular problems of your own industry must be presented. What is the nature of the competition you have to meet? How many plants are in competition with you? Where are they? What advantages do they possess over you, if any, in making or marketing their product? What is the total producing power of the country in your industry? What is the probable consuming power? All of the material can be graphically presented, like the Babsonchart, and explained in detail to employees.

Likewise, take up the prices of your product. What happened to them during the war? What has happened since? What is going to happen? Where must your prices be — what course must they take — in order for you to get business and keep the plant running? Take up the question of wages. What has been the course of wages in the country as a whole during the war and since? What has been the course of wages in your plant? How does this compare with the course of wages as a whole and with the course of wages in your competitor's plants?

What about the cost of living? The United States Bureau of Labor Statistics prepares regular reports on this subject. Have your employees seen them? Do they realize what these reports mean? Perhaps they do not believe that these reports are true. If that is the case, the thing for you to do is to have your employees join you in preparing local cost-of-living reports which they will accept as true.

So on all down the line. It may even be that you will find it to your advantage to go so far as to acquaint your employees with the profits, or losses, that you are making. Workers quite generally think that the boss is making a pile of money. For this reason, they do not accept at full value any pleas for wage reduction or increased efficiency that he may make. The balance sheet is the answer. Others have done it. Why not you? At any rate you can show them the unit production cost record. And if you can find a way to compare your own figures with those of your competitors, you will do well. Some of our industries which have effective associations have this material available.

I hope that *genuine profit sharing* has a great future ahead of it in the phase just begun. Notice that I say *genuine* profit sharing. Much of the prejudice against profit sharing comes from the fact that it has seldom been tried. There are relatively few real profit-sharing plants in the country. Profit sharing, to be genuine, must give to the employees a percentage, announced in advance, of the profits of the concern. Obviously, the percentage will fluctuate up or down with the profits. Obviously also, the profits must be known. The record of profits may well be posted each month or as often as the accounting system makes it feasible.

Have in mind what you are doing, or trying to do, with labor in this present stage of business. You are asking your employees to *work with you*. That is fundamentally different from asking them to *work for you*. If they are to work with you, it is but natural and reasonable that they have some of the same incentives that you yourself have. To say that the logic of profit sharing is loss sharing is aside from the point. Your employees are not working on the same margin as yourself. Even with profit sharing, they will not be rich. What among them is spread over a

large number, with you is divided up in most cases
among a few.   Still, it should be remembered that
there are a few cases where the employees have
joined loss sharing with profit sharing.   It merely
shows what can be done when the spirit is right.

By the time you have gone the distance which we
have thus far indicated, you will come to the place
where the dreaded efficiency system, which labor
usually hates like poison, with its stop watch and time
studies and speeding-up program, can be put in, with
the entire consent of the employees and with every
chance of success.   Thus, what Mr. Hoover's committee on waste has called to our attention can be
made available under the right conditions.   These
things have all been done; done under the old conditions.   They are not theoretical fancy.   The present
calls for them.   They are the way of salvation and
success in the times that we are now passing through.

The man who undertakes a movement like this
must be a man of real faith.   He must have faith in
human nature, as he finds it among his employees.
He must have faith in the wisdom of the plan.   And
he must be prepared to go the whole distance.   It is
idle to start upon a plan like this and stop half-way.
All of the cards must be laid on the table.   Absolute
candor and frankness are needed to-day in dealing
with labor.   Only thus will the reaction be genuine
and hearty.   Our men are ready to work with us,
just as soon as and to the extent that they find us
ready to work with them.

William Green, President of the American Federation of Labor, has said, " Co-operation is a very practical and natural policy. The tradition that the interests of management conflict with the interests of employees has been the cause of much waste in industry. If managements will only consider their losses from fighting their employees and spend equal thought and energy in earning their good-will, they will find the investment profitable.

" Standards of living can be permanently raised only by increasing the productivity of industry. The interests of American labor is focused upon securing an opportunity to help with the problems of this field. It is our hope the time will come when industrial relations problems will be decided in the conference room and industry will be convinced that real progress lies in co-operation to find more efficient methods."

Chapter IX

METHODS OF MARKETING

SOMETHING is wrong with the usual method of doing business; results prove it. Do you realize that the liabilities of failures equal — or exceed — losses from fires? Losses by fire for the last ten years were $4,264,492,000. For this same period liabilities of business failures were $4,293,-335,000.

What is the trouble? In my opinion it is due in large part to the excessive booms and the resulting disastrous panics; in other words, to these same fluctuations of business caused by lack of adjustment between production and distribution.

We have made tremendous strides in production, but we have lagged far behind in distribution. *If you compare production to the automobile, then distribution may be typified by the ox-cart.*

Do you realize what we have accomplished in production? In the making of boots and shoes, work which formerly by hand methods required nine hours requires but one by machinery. In the manufacture of laundry soap, work formerly requiring twenty hours now takes but one. Even greater savings occur with other articles. In making hammers or plows, where formerly about thirty-two hours were required, we now need but one hour. In the case of certain machine parts which can now be made in one hour the time required by hand methods was over 4,000 hours. The general average for all articles is about 250 to one. In other words, where by hand methods 250 hours of labor were required to produce a certain product, but one hour is now needed.

Compare this extraordinary advance in the efficiency of production with the corresponding development in distribution. It is absurd even to suggest that efficiency of distribution has been increased in anything like the ratio of 250 to one. In fact, from many standpoints, it may be questioned whether we have made any advance at all in distribution. I have at hand certain preliminary figures suggesting that there are various kinds of merchandise which cost more to market than to make. On a dollar article, for example, the cost to make may be expected to be 40 cents, and the cost to distribute, 60 cents. I have no doubt that even greater discrepancies might be found. What steps can we take to bring distribution and production more into alignment and correct adjustment? If we can find even a partial answer to this, we shall do much toward reducing the wild fluctuations of the business cycle.

We should bring to bear upon the problem of distribution the same scientific approach which has been so successfully applied to production. Selling has been largely a matter of guesswork, but we must place it squarely upon the foundation of facts first. As a concrete and specific example of what I mean by facts first, see the analysis at the close of this chapter. It is by no means complete, but it is suggested as a starting point. I should like to see every reader apply this analysis to his own business, or to work out a similar analysis.

After you have applied it certain facts will emerge. You will discover that you are selling or should sell primarily on the basis of industry. If you are making motor trucks, for example, you will find that your customers divide themselves into certain industrial groups, such as the iron and steel industry, the lumber industry, and so on through the dozen or more classifications of manufacturers and producers. If this is the way in which your business naturally aligns itself, then your distribution should be primarily based upon the study of industries. In another chapter this question of selling by industries has been considered at greater length.

In many instances, however, a business cannot well be classified by industry. For example, if you are selling food products, clothing, musical instruments, and other articles of final consumption, you will find that the more practical classification is by localities. Therefore, a separate chapter is devoted to this alternate problem of selling a city.

During the past few years I have studied and

analyzed both the plans and the results of several hundred sales and advertising campaigns — campaigns that succeeded and campaigns that failed. Detailed study of the latter indicates that at least 80 per cent. of those that fail do so, not because of a faulty plan or poor execution, but because they were builded upon a foundation of assumption, guesswork, or half truth instead of on sound fact. Millions in money and thousands of hours in earnest effort have been spent in a futile effort to sell mouth organs to deaf men.

As a small contribution to better business, I have prepared a standard merchandising analysis. We hope that it will help to eliminate this greatest cause of failure in marketing. It is simple and elemental. If time and money permit, we advise a much more extensive survey. In any case, however, an hour or two spent in examining your problem on the fifty points outlined will help to clarify it in your own mind and will tend to eliminate 50 per cent. of the chance for failure or half-hearted success. It is the most valuable hour you can put in on any sales or advertising problem.

Remember, FACTS FIRST — get the facts, or the facts will get you.

BABSON MERCHANDISING ANALYSIS

ECONOMIC FACTORS

Prospect

1. Who is your prospect?
   What is his or her position in the social and business world?
   Get as definite a description as you can of the man or woman you must sell.
2. How large is your market?
   Total number of prospects?
   Rate of growth or number of new prospects available each year?
3. Where are these prospects located?
   How many in each section of the country?
   Division by states if possible.
   Are the majority located in large cities, small towns, or rural and farming communities?
4. What is the prospect's relative prosperity?
   Income compared with a year ago?
   Relative position of the industry upon which he is dependent?
   In which month of the year is he most prosperous?
5. What portion of the market is already sold?
   How many of the possible prospects already buy from you regularly?
   What portion buy occasionally?
   How many do not buy at all?

Competition

6. What is being used now in place of your product or service?
   List competing articles or services.

7. Advantages of competition?
   List both apparent and real advantages of the competing articles or services.

8. Advantages over competition?
   List the advantages of your product or service over that of your competitor.

Distribution

9. Cost of product or service.
   (a) Cost of raw materials .... $————
   (b) Cost of labor and overhead cost .. $————
   (c) Total manufacturing cost .... $————
   (d) Selling cost .... $————
   (e) Profit .... $————
   (f) Selling price .... $————
   (g) Retail price .... $————

Tabulation of the costs where possible is very helpful. If labor and overhead cost, for instance, is much greater than the cost of the material, the price can in most cases be cut materially by volume production. In this case, it may be well to set low prices in order to get that volume. If material costs make up the largest portion of your manufacturing cost, volume is relatively unimportant, except in industries offering large discounts for quantity purchases of raw materials.

If your selling cost is larger than your total manufacturing cost, your price may be too high to be efficient. Be sure that a lower price would not sell enough more goods to increase the net profits, before you continue with a program that must overcome unusually high sales resistance.

Is your selling price determined by arriving at the manufacturing cost and adding all the traffic will bear, or is it decided by going to your market and finding out what the public wants to pay for your product? Neither of these processes

are entirely satisfactory. You should approach the problem
from both points of view and set a price somewhere between
the two extremes. Be sure that the margin between your selling price and the retail price is not too wide.

10. What is your plan of distribution?
      Which of the following factors do you employ in your
      scheme of distribution?
      (*a*) Mill agents or selling agents
      (*b*) Wholesalers
      (*c*) Jobbers
      (*d*) Retailers
      (*e*) Consumers
11. What are the avenues of distribution?
      Do you sell through branch offices, salesmen, direct by
      mail, or agents, exclusive or non-exclusive?
12 What are your terms to the customer?
      What discounts do you offer for cash?
      What is your credit policy?
      Do your discounts for quantity help in selling, or do
      they tend to overload your customer?
      How about dating?
      What is your policy regarding return goods?
      What guarantees are you willing to make and stand
      back of?

Psychological Factors

13. What are your fundamental appeals?
      Consider the following possible appeals and number in
      the order of importance in relation to your particular
      product or service:
      (*a*) Profit
      (*b*) Utility
      (*c*) Curiosity
      (*d*) Caution
      (*e*) Pride

14. Is your product known or unknown?

Is your prospect familiar with it or a similar article or service?

Does he already appreciate the need for it, or must he be educated to use it?

15. Is your product considered by the prospect as a luxury or essential?

16. Is your product or service of personal nature or for business use?

17. Have you the good will of the public?

Is your firm or product known or unknown?

Favorably or unfavorably known?

18. What is the present attitude of the prospect toward your product or service?

List all objections encountered in a sale.

List the points most easily understood, and those which require a more detailed explanation.

List any misapprehension of the public regarding your product or service.

19. Exactly what must the campaign accomplish?

If the product or service is known, and has features which are easily grasped by the public mind, a comparatively simple campaign should achieve the desired result. If, however, a good deal of educational work is necessary, a more extended plan will be required. Lay out a rough plan of the campaign that will be necessary.

Copy Factors

(For the preparation of both advertising and sales canvass)

20. What one point must the message convey?

No advertisement is large enough to contain two ideas. To insure unity, ask yourself what action is desired, and keep that definite idea in mind throughout the preparation of the advertisement or sales canvass.

21. Do the headline and illustration insure attention?

Will your copy be seen when competing with half a hundred other messages for the attention of your prospect?

Will your salesman's introduction insure a hearing for him?

22. Does the opening paragraph clinch interest?

Be sure that the message is presented from the prospect's point of view. Make certain that his advantage is emphasized rather than your own.

23. Does the message create a real desire to own or use the product or service advertised?

Desire is a feeling and is not a product of cold logic. Make your message breathe and live with illustration and description of the prospect enjoying the use of your merchandise.

24. Does the close outline clearly the action desired and urge to act quickly?

Be sure that you tell a man exactly what you want him to do, and make it easy for him to do it.

25. Does your copy carry a distinctive mark or style that will tie it up with your other efforts?

The accumulating effect of several different appeals is a tremendous force. Be sure that your messages are distinctive enough so that the prospect realizes that your product is the same product that he was reading about last month — that this is the machine, the equipment or service that he had already decided to buy.

26. Could the name of any other make or maker be substituted for your own?

If it can, your advertisement is completely worthless, except that it may do a certain amount of educational work for the good of the whole industry. You are advertising for the benefit of your competitor as well as yourself.

27. Is it completely free from meaningless slogans, insignificant trademarks, and useless words?

These examples of literary deadwood not only take up valuable and expensive space and make the message's work long and hard to read, but they actually befog and confuse the mind of the reader, so that he is left with a very indistinct impression of what you are trying to tell him. Write as though it cost a dollar a word.

28. Does the copy ring true?

When completed read your copy.

Does it sound as if it were in earnest?

Does it make empty claims or does it offer evidence and proof?

If it offers no proof, it will convince no one.

Will the product fulfill the promise?

If not, improve the product.

Display Factors — Sample Cases

29. Can the prospect see it?

In making up the salesmen's sample cases, it is well to remember that the eye is much quicker than the ear. Samples that the prospect can look at, handle, or work are better than the most eloquent description ever written. If you cannot put your samples in the salesman's hands, be sure that he is provided with sample charts and photographs that will tell the story.

Publications

30. What is the circulation?

Where is it located geographically?

What per cent. of the readers are prospects?

Cost per page, per thousand for reaching prospects?

Magazines offer a splendid medium for educational work, where the percentage of prospects is large enough to make them worth while.

31. Trade publications.

If you are interested in reaching a certain line of business, trade publications offer a circulation without waste. The cost in this case should be compared with the problem of a direct mail campaign to cover the same field.

32. Newspapers.

The largest and most inexpensive circulation in the United States, offering an unusual opportunity to cultivate certain localities. Positions in the various sections of the paper offer still further chances to appeal to a definite class. Percentage of prospects should again decide the practicability of this medium.

33. A poster display.

Outdoor bulletins and street car cards offer valuable space if your product is of general use.

34. Direct mail.

By selection of a mailing list this medium can be used without any waste circulation. It should be the backbone of any campaign which is to concentrate on a limited number of prospects, and should be used in conjunction with regular publication advertising in the follow up and cultivation of interested prospects.

The duplicated letter offers the most elastic and practical form where there is no need of detailed description. In the more elaborate presentations the details should be covered in a printed folder or booklet which accompanies the letter. Whenever possible illustrate the product and show it in use. The possibilities for variety in direct mail material are almost unlimited. Handled intelligently, it offers unusual possibilities for efficient marketing.

35. Dealers' helps.

Window display.

Counter stands.

Samples and other forms of advertising, which can be placed in the dealer's store, or presented to the public through him are of tremendous effect, and ordinarily the cost is little more than the actual preparation of the material itself. The space used is donated by the dealer, and the final advantage is that the appeal is made where the goods are easily accesible and can be procured without delay.

36.   Miscellaneous.

There are a score of more or less minor classifications in the medium field, including novelties, exhibitions, demonstrations, and displays, and other particular forms which are adopted to serve in a limited field. These should be considered as accessory and auxiliary forces and should not be depended upon to carry the heavy end of the sales message.

Physical Form

37.   Type.

It is well to stick to a few of the better-known type faces. Fancy types are hard to read. Small type spaced out is better than large type jammed together. Get your emphasis by the use of *italics* and SMALL CAPS, rather than by trying to mix several of these families of type into a single layout.

38.   Illustration.

Make the picture mean something. Make it emphasize a single point. Make it help sell. Explain the purpose of the advertisement, and a good commercial artist will know what form of handling will best serve your purpose. Money spent for effective illustration is well invested.

39.   Color.

In preparing printed matter the limited use of color has

a very constructive force. It is better to use too little than too much. Don't slap it on with a trowel.

40. Paper.

Paper should be selected for the work it is to do, not by the price per pound. Each of the several grades has a purpose. If you are not familiar with the different papers, get a good printer and let him select the right sheet for your particular case.

NOTE — Wherever possible it is imperative that the campaign be tested on a limited field of prospects before it is adopted. The observance of this rule in conjunction with a careful survey will practically eliminate the chance of failure.

CHAPTER X

SELLING A CITY

IF your products are consumer's goods, that is, bought by the general public rather than any particular group or industry, it is safe to say that your marketing plan should be built for the city as a unit. If you are in the retail business, obviously you must operate on this unit; but if you are doing a national business you can readily increase your sales efficiency by following the same plan.

Conditions are not alike in any two cities at one time, and sales possibilities in adjoining localities may differ by as wide a margin as 50 to 60 per cent. It is ridiculous, therefore, to assume that the campaign designed to sell the country as a whole will be 100 per cent. productive in each of these various communities under all of these different circumstances. It is safe to say that sales can be increased 10 to 30 per cent. on every dollar you spend in advertising and sales effort, if you will take the trouble to study each city and fit your plans to local conditions, whatever they may be.

Here are a few of the things that decide the difference between success and failure, between profit and loss:

St. Louis, for example. How many salesmen
should you put into St. Louis? Can you adequately
cover this city with two men, or three, or four, or
a dozen, or how many? Should these men be traveling salesmen or resident salesmen? If a resident,
should they have desk-room only or a well-equipped
sales office? Or — another thought — can your
products be adequately distributed in St. Louis by
mail? Going to the other extreme, how about a
warehouse in connection with the sales office? How
about dealers — their number, their volume of business, their probable sales of your particular product? Again, is St. Louis the kind of a city you
can count upon for a long pull and profitably spend
years in developing, or is it more like a mining camp
or oil town — fit only to be plucked quickly while
the plucking is good? Is the present a favorable
time to approach the St. Louis market or will it be
more responsive at a later date?

These are typical questions applying to any city
or state and occurring constantly in an active sales
department. The credit department has a similar
set of questions. Should credit in St. Louis be extended liberally, guardedly, or practically not at all?
Should collection efforts be mild, medium, or
drastic? Of course, it all depends on the local outlook. Your credit and collection policies depend on
whether St. Louis is on the eve of profound depression or about to enjoy a record-breaking prosperity. Then comes the advertising department

with its own particular questions. How much newspaper advertising and other forms of publicity will
St. Louis repay? Or if a local campaign has already
been run and recorded, is the score good, bad, or
indifferent?

There are always two questions about a locality:
first, the question of those who are contemplating
the field as prospective territory; second, the question of those already located therein and desiring to
check up past records or formulate future policies
of advertising, selling, credit granting, and collecting. Both questions depend upon a precise knowledge of the local situation and outlook. Many business concerns will not take the trouble to get this
knowledge. They are governed as the old-fashioned, one-cylinder gasoline engine was governed
— by the " hit or miss " method. This will not be
admitted by some sales managers, advertising men,
and credit men, who claim they are operating, not
by luck and chance, but by intuition.

Intuition is a wonderful thing — when it works.
I have a great respect for it — when it works. But
it doesn't always work. Intuition is what prompts
a hen to sit on china eggs as optimistically as on the
real article. Intuition is what tempts the setter pup
to point at the parrot cage. Intuition is what leads
many business men into the embrace of the receiver.

In his book, " The Friendly Arctic," Stefansson
makes this significant remark:

When I am lost in a storm, or when I am in doubt of any kind I frequently find that my feelings, or so-called " instincts," are in conflict with deliberate reason, and I have invariably found that the " instincts" are unreliable. I may have the strongest feeling, which almost amounts to a conviction, that my camp lies in a certain direction, for example, when a careful review of circumstances shows that it really ought to lie in another.

If " hunch " is a treacherous guide in polar exploration it is even more so in dealing with the complex problems of business.

Those who realize the need for definite data as the footings of success usually turn first to population statistics. Population statistics are always better than nothing. But they have certain radical defects. The U. S. Census enumeration is made only at intervals of ten years and even then the full returns are not published promptly. Certain estimates are made yearly, but often fail to include various localities on which data are important, such as places losing population.

Another weakness in population figures is their arbitrary character. Rarely do the political boundaries of a city coincide with its true economic or business boundaries. Take Boston, for example. Politically, Boston includes Roxbury but not Brookline, Dorchester but not Newton, Charlestown but not Chelsea. Or compare San Francisco with Los Angeles. The political boundaries of San Francisco are narrowly drawn and its population is proportionately small.   But the political boundaries of Los Angeles are widely drawn and its population is proportionately large.   You will appreciate the absurdity of accepting population figures as a measure of a city's business magnitude, by noting the following fact: For most of the leading cities the business area or trading area has a population anywhere from 2 to 100 per cent. greater than the population of the city proper, or the political area.

Assume, however, that you have obtained corrected or true population figures.   You are still far from a measurement of the locality's real purchasing power.   Purchasing power cannot be judged by population alone.   To the census enumerator, all people look alike.

The successful seller of merchandise cannot follow merely census figures.   A man may be a man and still not be a prospective customer.   The decisive factor is purchasing power.   A man who is spending $2 offers double the market offered by the man who is spending $1.   *In a business sense, the important thing is not people but pocketbooks.*

We now come to the central problem of all distribution, namely: the forecast of purchasing power. The statistical highways and byways are strewn with wrecks of formulas which have been devised for the appraisal of purchasing power.   To make such a formula is as easy as rolling off a log — and of as much commercial value.   You start with population, then you deduct Negro population — forget the fact that when a Negro is in funds, as thousands of them are in a period of high-priced cotton, he is one of the most generous customers known to scientific merchandising. However, a sordid and mercenary point of this kind is distasteful to the formula hound. Something must be done with the Negro; so deduct him. Some authorities favor deducting also whites of foreign or mixed parentage between assigned age limits or resident in specified localities. By this time the formula hound is really warmed up and hitting on all twelve cylinders. He squares the number of radio outfits located in the city, extracts the cube root of local " hooch " mills — of foreign or mixed parentage — divides the quotient by the remainder plus three times the mayor's salary.

Now all this statistical " jazz " is great stuff to show the visiting delegates to some annual convention of mouth-organ manufacturers, but for real service it doesn't mean much. From a business standpoint any measurement of a city's sales possibilities must answer two tests: (1) it must be simple; (2) it must be up to date, preferably more than up to date — a trend.

Simplicity and foresight, these are the cardinal virtues of any attempt to appraise a city's capacity as a market for your products. The problem has never been stated more succinctly than in the following letter in which an automobile manufacturer lays down the A B C of territorial appraisal:

I want to get a more practical method of sizing up a city than by hunch and hope. I want to control distribu-

tion by actual figures the same as I control production.
Now if these figures are to be of real service to us they
must meet certain specifications.   Here are the specifications:

The figures must be real rather than some theoretical
abstraction; we want actual, specific, and concrete data that
our men can understand.

The figures must be more than historical.   We want,
not only a record of the past, but also a guide to the future.

At the outset of this discussion it was noted that
any measurement of a territory's business activity
or purchasing power must be capable of extension
into the future.   This is manifestly the crucial point
of the entire program.   It is the outlook rather than
the situation which interests the business man.   The
historian is interested in the past, the newspaper is
interested in the present, but the business man is
interested in the future.   For example, in such a
time as the early part of 1920, New England was
booming — no question about it.   " Present conditions " really were excellent.   Business men who regarded only present conditions, made heavy commitments based thereon. But business men who regarded the future saw trouble ahead and put their
houses in order.

Again, in the latter part of the same year, when
the slump in the Northeast had created a general
attitude of gloom and apprehension, many business
men thought that the Pacific Coast was destined for
immediate reaction. Those who specialized on the
future however, were not pessimistic because they

knew that the Pacific Coast is slow to participate in a depression just as it is slow to participate in prosperity. It is one of those sections which "lag," using this word in a technical sense. Scores of illustrations could be cited to show that a city's present status gives no clue to what local policies should be followed. These are indicated only by a forecast.

Attempting to forecast the short swings of the stock market — the day-to-day or week-to-week movements — is rank speculation. Reputable economists and statisticians do not countenance such forecasts. The same applies to gambling in the cotton and grain markets, a common practice in some localities. Buying securities or commodities for actual needs, however, is perfectly legitimate. So also is the process of hedging used by millers and others to insure a definite margin of profit on orders for future delivery. Forecasting the business activity that will prevail in a city in a given period 60 to 90 days in the future, is likewise both legitimate and necessary.

Such a forecast is exactly what all successful executives should make in order to determine what shall be the output for the year, to schedule production, to take advantage of long-range buying, to stabilize labor forces, to facilitate financial plans, and to make selling and advertising plans. A distributor is necessarily forced to set some sort of quota. This quota should be an index of the territory's real possibilities and not an arbitrary measure of past performance. A forecast of this kind is a necessary and legitimate business risk.

For several years the more alert and far-sighted executives have been keenly interested in picking localities which have the most favorable outlook. In a general way these executives have been able to foresee the trend of business in their various territories. Recently, however, there have been developed more definite methods, and fairly precise forecasts of local business conditions can be made several months in advance. It seems at first thought a most difficult undertaking, but the same could have been said of any other step in science. Moreover, with a growing fund of data on leading cities the well-organized statistical department should be in a better position to make these local forecasts than is the general executive whose attention is demanded by countless other activities.

In preparing such forecasts it is imperative to make the most thorough analysis possible of conditions affecting the local outlook in each city. Find out what has been the trend of local business during recent years, during recent months, or even during the past week. In other words, determine the present position of the city in the economic trend.

From studies extended back over a period of years, you can ascertain what the normal seasonal tendencies of business are in each city from month to month. Finally you can list the basic industries or factors that determine the prosperity or purchasing power of the city, and the relative order of their importance. It is a question of foreseeing the future of the raw materials and manufactured products upon which local prosperity depends — modified by seasonal and secular trends.

Charts " A " and " B " suggest some of the material used in making a forecast for the city of Atlanta.

Chart " A " shows the movement of business in Atlanta during the post-war boom, the subsequent reaction, and the later trend. The study of the sales figures of a large number of organizations as well as the official figures of retail and wholesale trade indicate that this chart is an extremely precise indicator.

Chart " B " shows the increase or decline in business that should take place from one month to the next in an average year. This chart of seasonal tendencies is made from a study of figures covering a period of ten years. (Practically no change is made in such a chart by taking a twenty-year period instead of a ten-year period.)

Here are the factors determining the purchasing power of Atlanta: cotton goods, 30 per cent. of all manufactured products; cottonseed products, 6 per cent.; fertilizer, 5 per cent.; printing and publishing, 3 per cent.; clothing, 3 per cent.; all other industries, 53 per cent.; cotton, 41 per cent. of all crops; corn, 31 per cent.; hay, 6 per cent.; all other crops, 22 per cent. Next in importance are mining

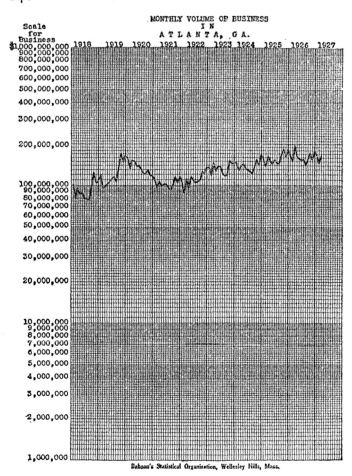

CHART A

and quarrying, and lumbering in nearby territory. The above list indicates that local industries are

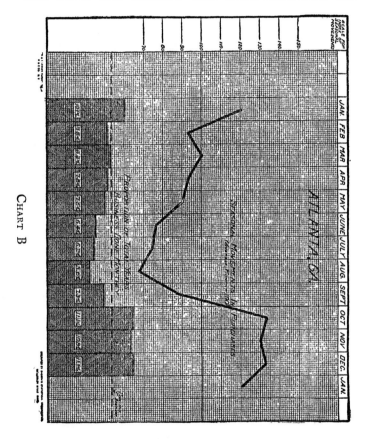

CHART B

somewhat more important than agriculture. Of the industries, cotton manufacturing is far in the lead

and is the one that should receive the greatest consideration. Of the crops, cotton and corn are the
only ones we need consider.

In using these charts to make a forecast, " A "
would be brought up to date and projected two
months into the future, according to the seasonal
tendencies brought out by Chart " B." In an average year this is the path that business would follow,
and if this line alone were used to make a forecast,
the results would not often be far astray. In actual
practice, however, it is best to change the slope of
this line according as the average outlook for local
raw materials and finished products is for a seasonal
movement more or less pronounced than usual. If,
for example, the seasonal tendency is upward during
the period under consideration but the readjustment
process is just gathering momentum, the projected
line would be inclined less sharply or might even
be bent forward. This, of course, depends upon
the city and the position of its industries.

In a city like New York, movements are very
gradual and even a general period of readjustment
does not result in a radical change in the trend of
the business line. On the other hand, a city that is
closely associated with agriculture, usually has very
pronounced seasonal movements. In the latter case,
forecasts made when the influence of the business is
depressing the price of farm products should allow
for only a minor " seasonal rise."

The situation differs for each city under consideration and a record of what has taken place in the past is absolutely essential. Of course, such a record is not completely comprehensive; neither is the forecast infallible. It has been abundantly demonstrated, however, that off-hand estimates which do not take into consideration the position of a city in the economic cycle, seasonal tendencies, and the outlook for basic industries, may carry one far astray.

The proof of the pudding is in the eating. Chart " C " shows in bull's-eye form the results of an actual forecast for the month of February in a given year. This forecast was made 90 days in advance, early in November of the preceding year, and 100 cities were checked. The actual February statistics showed that 55 per cent. of the estimates came within 5 points; 79 per cent., within 10 points; and 94 per cent., within 15 points. This particular forecast was selected at random.

It is not composed of " statistical " conclusions entirely, nor is it mainly the expression of an individual opinion. It comprises the intelligent application of sound business judgment to statistical research and takes into consideration the characteristics peculiar to local conditions.

A convenient form for arranging such a forecast is as follows:

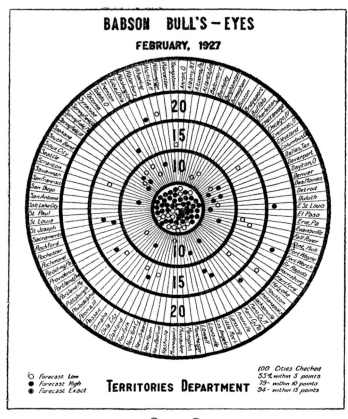

CHART C

EXPECTATION OF BUSINESS
100 = Same Month of Preceding Year
Feb.

Akron, Ohio	95	Fort Worth, Tex.	130
Albany, N. Y.	100	Harrisburgh, Pa.	105
Altoona, Pa.	105	Hartford, Conn.	105
Atlanta, Ga.	95	Holyoke, Mass.	85
Baltimore, Md.	90	Houston, Tex.	105
Berkeley, Cal.	110	Indianapolis, Ind.	120
Binghamton, N. Y.	105	Jacksonville, Fla.	95
Birmingham, Ala.	100	Kansas City, Kan.	105
Boston, Mass.	105	Kansas City, Mo.	110
Bridgeport, Conn.	105	Knoxville, Tenn.	100
Buffalo, N. Y.	100	Lansing, Mich.	105
Charleston, S. C.	110	Little Rock, Ark.	110
Chattanooga, Tenn.	110	Los Angeles, Cal.	110
Chicago, Ill.	105	Louisville, Ky.	105
Cincinnati, Ohio	100	Lowell, Mass.	100
Cleveland, Ohio	105	Manchester, N. H.	90
Columbus, Ohio	100	Milwaukee, Wis.	105
Dallas, Tex.	105	Minneapolis, Minn.	90
Davenport, Ia.	115	Mobile, Ala.	100
Dayton, Ohio	110	Nashville, Tenn.	100
Denver, Colo.	105	New Bedford, Mass.	90
Des Moines, Ia.	110	New Haven, Conn.	105
Detroit, Mich.	100	New Orleans, La.	90
Duluth, Minn.	80	New York, N. Y.	105
E. St. Louis, Ill.	115	Norfolk, Va.	115
El Paso, Tex.	95	Oakland, Cal.	115
Erie, Pa.	110	Oklahoma City, Okla.	115
Evansville, Ind.	110	Omaha, Nebr.	95
Fall River, Mass.	95	Passaic, N. J.	100
Flint, Mich.	120	Peoria, Ill.	105
Fort Wayne, Ind.	95	Philadelphia, Pa.	100

Pittsburgh, Pa. 100
Portland, Me. . . . . ,.. . . 100
Portland, Ore. 110
Providence, R. I. 95
Reading, Pa. 100
Richmond, Va. . . . ., 95|
Rochester, N. Y. 100
Rockford, Ill. 115
Sacramento, Cal. 105
St. Joseph, Mo. 105
St. Louis, Mo. 100
St. Paul, Minn. 95
Salt Lake City, Utah . . . 100
San Antonio, Tex. 110
San Diego, Cal. 110
San Francisco, Cal. 105
Savannah, Ga. 105
Scranton, Pa. . . ,.. 110
Seattle, Wash. 105
Sioux City, Ia. . . . . . ,.. . 95
South Bend, Ind. 105

Spokane, Wash. . . .. :.. . .. 105
Springfield, Ill. . . . ., 95
Springfield, Mass. 105
Springfield, Ohio 110
Syracuse, N. Y. 105
Tacoma, Wash. 100
Toledo, Ohio 110
Trenton, N. J. ,. 100
Tulsa, Okla. 115
Washington, D. C. 105
Waterbury, Conn. 125
Wheeling, W. Va. 105
Wichita, Kan. 105
Wilmington, Del. 115
Worcester, Mass. . . . . .,. 100
Youngstown, Ohio . . . . ., 100

United States
  Excl. N. Y. C. 105
  Total U. S. . . ,.. . .,.. . 105

The usefulness of such forecasts to national and regional distributors is obvious. But with the continued application of the scientific approach to business problems, it is possible that a local forecast will be of even greater utility to the retailer. If you are a retailer you should have each month a forecast (ninety days in advance) of the business activity of your city. For example, in May, forecast August business. A figure of 110 per cent., say, indicates that in August your city's business will be 10 per cent. better than in August of last year. A figure of 95 per cent. means that in August your city's business will be 5 per cent. less than in August of last year. In each case August of last year is taken as the base, or 100. The forecast refers to business as expressed in terms of dollars rather than physical units.

Estimate the coming demand. Knowing what your sales were in August of last year, and multiplying this figure by the percentage forecast for your city, you can readily get a close estimate of what your sales should be this coming August. Actual records show that an improvement in general business conditions is followed by a corresponding increase in retail sales, and a general decline is followed by a decline in retailing. Having estimated in this way your volume of August sales, you can gauge your stocks of merchandise so that you can take advantage of the demand. At the same time you avoid the danger of having a great quantity of unsold goods left on your hands.

Aid your financing. In some instances you may wish to borrow at your bank to finance purchases of merchandise. The forecast for your city should be of distinct value in this connection. When a considerable improvement in business is indicated, this favorable outlook should be brought to the attention of your banker, just as you would show him your statement. Moreover, from your own standpoint, you want your loans to be accurately adjusted to the business outlook. It is no advantage to a merchant to burden himself with heavier obligations than sales prospects warrant. On the other hand, he desires sufficient credit to avail himself of any improvement in sight. The amount of accommodation most advantageous depends upon the amount of prosperity ahead — and this is measured by the forecast figure. Bank and borrower alike have a common interest in correctly ascertaining the trend, and an accurate local forecast is for the benefit of both.

Handle your employment problem with an eye to the future. No merchant cares to have an oversupply of sales people and clerical workers. Nor does he want to incur the ill will of customers by failing to give adequate service. The whole employment problem, therefore, makes it necessary to predetermine the demand. If August is going to find your store thronged with customers, you will need a larger staff than you would were trade to be moderate.   A correct forecast will help you in laying out your personal requirements ninety days in advance.

Look ahead when shaping advertising policy. Judging by statistics of local newspaper advertising, most stores prefer to advertise more liberally when the trend is upward.   There is room for argument on this point, but assuming that a merchant wants to enlarge his publicity of all kinds if business is due for expansion, a local forecast figure gives him a dependable compass.   Moreover, an accurate anticipation of conditions will aid in deciding not only the amount of the advertising appropriation but also the character of the advertising appeal.   When business is on the upgrade the public readily respond to arguments which fall flat during the stress of hard times.

Merchandise to meet the times.   Of course this same principle of writing advertising to fit conditions applies also to other parts of merchandising. The selection of goods, the education of sales people, window dressing, counter displays — every side of the business depends on meeting the public mood. Practices which were eminently successful during the boom were disastrous during the ensuing depression, and a further revision will be necessary to capitalize the approaching revival.

To forecast business conditions is to forecast the

needs and desires of the public; and to forecast and adequately meet these public needs and desires is to succeed in retailing.   Public needs and desires act in accordance with economic law.   The law of action and reaction determines what the public will need and desire in the months to come.   A correct knowledge of present conditions and the application of the law is essential to successful merchandising.

Chapter XI

SELLING AN INDUSTRY

VERY few sales organizations reach, either in their advertising or selling activities, all the people or business concerns that are logical sales prospects. Moreover, only the most up-to-date and well-managed concerns keep informed regarding changes in the condition of their customers' businesses. Alert sales managers are to-day eagerly developing important lines of market information that have heretofore been given but scant consideration.

There are various ways of selling open to sales organizations. Some concerns handling a product which is judged to have a nation-wide market broadcast advertising matter all over the country. This advertising is placed in newspapers and periodicals of all kinds in the hope that it will reach the eye of a prospective purchaser. This, of course, is more or less of a blind way of going at the proposition. Unless the concern is so fortunate as to have hit upon a particularly prosperous time throughout the country, such methods of selling are bound to be costly.

As pointed out in Chapter X, many concerns endeavor to direct their selling efforts toward selected cities, towns, or other geographical divisions. The idea is to pick out those sections where business is best and concentrate advertising and selling activities on them. This method is much better than the one mentioned above. By ignoring localities where purchasing power is small or temporarily below normal, both time and money are saved.

The concerns that are most successful are those that know the most about their prospective customers.

These concerns not only ascertain certain kinds of people or business firms that constitute their market, but they also keep in touch with the condition of each customer's business. They know how big a buyer they are catering to; they know when his business is active and when it is dull; and they know when his purchasing power is high and when it is poor. In other words, they have a finger on the pulse of their market at all times. The selling expense of such organization is very low compared to others.

If you are one of those who have made no special study of your market but have been working along on a basis of experience and tradition, you are not making the most of your opportunities. If you have been confining your campaign studies to the selection of prosperous localities only, you are even then not making the most of your opportunities. You are still laboring under needless risks, worries, and losses.

Regardless of whether you are a wholesale distributor in many localities, or a retailer doing business in only one locality, you can increase your sales and reduce your selling expense substantially by directing your advertising and sales forces to meet changing conditions in the industries to which you desire to sell or which employ your customers.

If your product is classed as equipment, machinery, supplies, or services of interest only to a certain class or group of industries, information as to the present condition and future outlook for those industries should be in hand before you spend a single dollar or send out a single salesman in an effort to market your product. If your line is highly specialized, cotton machinery for instance, you must sell to a single industry and your sales and advertising campaigns should be undertaken only after securing the latest information and forecasts of the cotton goods industry.

If your product is one that can be sold to several different lines, office furniture or electrical equipment, for example, you will find that a campaign laid out and directed to each industry individually will lower your cost of distribution substantially. You have an opportunity to cut your sales expenses from 10 to 30 per cent., and if you happen to be in a mail order field you can cut even more.

If, instead of being a wholesaler you are a retailer whose market is limited to a given city, you also can profit by a knowledge of what is going on in the various industries, of what their rate of producing activity is, and of whether or not they are prosperous and employing normal amounts of labor. A retailer can put such information to a very practical use. It is true that thousands of retailers do not know the lines of business in which their customers are engaged. Nevertheless, you can ascertain easily the kind of industries that are employing people in your city or town, and by studying present conditions and the future outlook for these industries, you can decide which classes of your possible customers are now the most prosperous and which are going to be.

Always in every city, some one or more industries are prosperous. The merchant who studies business fundamentals will make his business immensely more profitable by directing his sales drives toward the people engaged in those lines.

Cater to these classes by directing your advertising in the local papers towards them and by stocking up with goods that that class of people are in the habit of calling for. In this way, you will be conducting your business along the lines of least resistance, and will, without question, increase your sales and obtain a quicker turnover on your stock. Up-to-date retail sales managers have increased their sales very markedly by directing their advertising in this manner and by catering especially and directly to people engaged in industries that were known to be prosperous.

Retailers of any article or line of goods, bond salesmen, insurance and real estate men, will all find increased profits by directing their selling activities toward the people who have the cash to buy.

Wholesaler or retailer, when your sales efforts are based on a statistical knowledge of your customer's business, when all wasted effort is eliminated by directing your energies straight to the concern or individual with the buying power, then you are selling scientifically.

If you are selling some product to only one or a few industries, it may be well for you to consider whether or not you are selling to all of the industries that could use your product. To those who desire to broaden their sales field, an analysis of the industrial market will reveal rich possibilities.

Strange as it may seem, sellers do not realize all of the ways in which their product can be used. We have many times been informed by some manufacturer or salesman in a rather humorous vein that so-and-so " has discovered a new use for my product." With changing conditions in the various industries whereby new processes are replacing old, new products being tried out, etc., it behooves the manufacturer of any product to keep a watchful eye on the developments in the entire industrial layout.

There are over 300 different kinds of manufacturing industries in the country. These industries comprise over 187,000 establishments employing over

8,000,000 wage earners. **From the abrasive industry** at the alphabetical top of the list to woven goods at the bottom, there is embraced a wide variety of business activity. These 187,000 manufacturing establishments buy nearly $36,000,000,000 of goods each year. They purchase raw materials, equipment, and supplies of every conceivable kind.

The following table shows how the annual purchases of the various major groups of industries compare with each other:

ANNUAL PURCHASES BY GROUPS OF INDUSTRIES

Industry	*Amount of Purchases*
Food and kindred products	$7,748,678,000
Textiles and their products	5,348,050,000
Chemicals and allied products	4,180,411,000
Iron and steel and their products not including machinery	3,734,350,000
Transportation equipment, air, land, and water	3,389,101,000
Metals and metal products, other than iron and steel	1,946,777,000
Machinery, not including transportation equipment	1,935,367,000
Lumber and allied products	1,724,983,000
Paper, printing, and related industries	1,614,235,000
Leather and its manufactures	1,015,123,000
Rubber products	718,840,000
Stone, clay, and glass products	603,427,000
Railroad repair shops	563,646,000
Tobacco manufactures	425,769,000
Musical instruments and phonographs	98,761,000
Miscellaneous industries	833,630,000
Total	$35,881,148,000

INDUSTRIES

INDUSTRIES	JAN	FEB	MAR	APR	MAY	JUN	JUL	AUG	SEP	OCT	NOV	DEC
AUTOMOBILE												
BOOT & SHOE												
BRICK												
CANNING												
CEMENT												
CLOTHING (MEN'S)												
CONFECTIONERY												
COTTON GOODS												
ELECTRICAL EQUIPMENT												
FERTILIZER												
FOUNDRY												
FUR GOODS												
JEWELRY												
PAINT & VARNISH												
PAPER												
PHONOGRAPH												
SILK GOODS												
TIRE												
TOY												
WOOLEN GOODS												

When examining the industrial market with a view to deciding upon a selling field, attention should be paid to two very desirable features of a market; namely, (1) breadth, and (2) seasonal uniformity. The broader the field, the less likelihood there is of losses due to the troubles that afflict single industries from time to time, such as overproduction and strikes. The concern with only one customer is not in so secure a position as the concern with one hundred, notwithstanding that the one concern may be buying fully as much as the entire hundred. There is more safety in a diversified market. And the market that holds up well in all seasons is obviously a more profitable one than a one or two-season market. In the former case, manufacturing is done much more efficiently, both producing and selling organizations are more stable, and less business risk is involved in the handling of inventories.

The thing to do, therefore, is to study the seasonal habits of the various industries and determine the time of year in which each usually encounters its season of greatest manufacturing activity. (See accompanying chart.) By timing sales and advertising campaigns to anticipate manufacturers' seasonal requirements for equipment, materials, and supplies in selected industries, it is possible to maintain a fairly uniform market throughout every season of the year.

It may be that in order to carry out this plan of

a year-around market, it will be necessary to handle more than one product. For example, the seller of wire screens required for building purposes largely in the spring and summer should take on some line that is associated with the heating and ventilating of industrial buildings and business quarters in the winter.

The first step, then, in determining what industries form a possible market for your product is to examine the activities of the various industries in the light of the possible ways in which your article or commodity can reasonably be expected to be used. This will necessitate a clear understanding of the merits of your own product and a knowledge of the nature of the activity of the various industries.

In order to acquire a knowledge of the nature of the activity of the various industries, information must be secured showing the kind of products being produced and the layout of plant and equipment used to manufacture and sell them. The size of the various concerns in any industry should be ascertained and the quantities of materials, supplies, and equipment required by each estimated.

A study of the above kind will frequently reveal a number of hitherto unsuspected customers among the industries. However, whether you sell to one industry or many, whether you sell direct to the manufacturer or to his employees, you should be in possession of the facts concerning present conditions and the future outlook in each.

How will you go about analyzing the purchasing power of your customers? Which ones will be the most active and the readiest buyers? Will all concerns in any one industry be equally good customers? How long will the prosperous concerns continue active? All these questions will arise constantly. You can answer them by keeping in touch with fundamental business conditions and by watching the special factors which are peculiar to the various individual industries.

In the first place, all industries are influenced by the varying phases of business. As already stated in a previous chapter, industrial history has always consisted of distinct phases and although of different duration, each phase has consisted of four periods; namely, (1) a period of over-expansion, (2) a period of decline, (3) a period of depression, and (4) a period of improvement. These periods follow one another by reason of the natural reaction of economic conditions. The idea that reckless expansion can ever become an actual fact and not be followed by a business depression is a fallacy.

All that is borrowed must be repaid, and as long as business insists upon over-drawing its account, we must expect the consequent reaction.

In order to study fundamental business conditions, statistics regarding bank clearings, business failures, building permits, commodity prices, production of basic raw materials, employment, foreign trade, money rates, etc., must be collected and correlated. These statistics will indicate when general business is in a prosperous condition and when it is in a depressed condition. They will also tell when it is time to expect a long swing improvement in business, and conversely, when to expect a long swing decline.

It is improbable for the manufacturing activity of all the industries to vary exactly in unison with general business as indicated by statistics of fundamental barometers. Most industries either lag behind or precede the general movement. Changes in the business cycle do not cause the same degree of change in the manufacturing activity of every industry. Special factors peculiar to each industry are responsible for this lack of complete uniformity.

Between the turning point in a period of depression and the turning point in a period of prosperity, when demand is improving, prices rising faster than costs, profits good, failures declining and many new concerns entering business, the manufacturing activity of most industries is usually strong. On the other hand, between the turning point in a period of prosperity and the turning point in a period of depression, when demand is declining, prices receding below the cost of production, losses mounting, and failures increasing, most of the industries are forced to adopt a policy of curtailment and purchase very little. It is very important, therefore, to study and watch the changing phases of business independently of the various conditions

AN INDUSTRIAL ANALYSIS

FURNITURE INDUSTRY COMPARED WITH
ALL INDUSTRIES

SCALE	1922	1923	1924	1925	1926	1927	SCALE
INDEX							INDEX

FURNITURE

ALL INDUSTRIES

BABSON'S

120   110   100   90

which are peculiar to any one industry.

Do not, however, ignore the special conditions affecting any given industry. We must look carefully into the demand it is receiving for its product, both in the domestic market and from abroad. We must examine carefully statistics showing the way in which supply is changing due to variations in producing activity, in the rate of importation, and in the amount of stocks held for sale. We must be especially careful to study the way in which the cost of production is changing and the factors responsible for such changes. The price of the industry's product and the various factors that will tend either to increase or decrease it must be looked into. In the case of any particular concern, the competition which that concern is meeting will be a factor in its sales. All of these economic conditions change frequently and bring about changes in the purchasing activity of the industry.

We must also consider certain other factors which usually have an influence on the outlook for an industry, namely, the labor situation, the transportation situation, money conditions, the crops, the tariff, and the trend of legislation.

In making a study of the probable purchasing activity of an industry, the particular thing we must watch is the way in which the above factors affect the rate of manufacturing in the various establishments. The more active manufacturing is, the more materials, equipment, and supplies will be needed.

Sometimes a manufacturing establishment will continue to manufacture when profits are practically zero. Nevertheless, even then it will need to buy raw materials and supplies if it wishes to avoid shutting down. Hence, the point we have to consider is how to anticipate changes in manufacturing activity.

As a preliminary step, it will be well to obtain an over-all idea of the industry. The first questions that naturally arise have to do with the usefulness of the industry's products and the reasons for the establishment of the industry in its present centers. The age of the industry, and the rate of its past growth, also its relative importance compared with other industries should be ascertained. In this connection, we should recognize and give due weight to the fact that the permanency of the industry will depend on the continued usefulness of its product and its continued ability to combine the necessary elements of production and distribution. The usefulness of carriages and wagons is beginning to wane due to the advent of the automobile. The manufacture of wooden automobile wheels is giving way to the manufacture of steel wheels because of increasing difficulty in obtaining hickory.

Let us consider first how changes in the demand for your customer's product will cause changes in his desire or ability to purchase the thing you wish to sell him. When his demand is good and he is actively producing, he will buy raw materials, supplies, and equipment of various kinds. Conversely, when his demand declines, he will curtail production and will be less likely to buy. If he happens to be in the jewelry industry, for example, you will find that the number of people who desire to buy jewelry is much greater during periods of prosperity than during periods of depression because the purchasing power of the public is generally stronger when times are good than when times are hard. In general, the higher the price of jewelry advances, the harder it will be to sell it because there will be fewer people with the necessary purchasing power. Conversely, the lower the price of jewelry declines, the more people there will be in a position to buy it. Hence, the purchasing activity of any industry will, all other things remaining constant, rise and fall with increases and decreases in the demand for its product.

Another important item to inquire into is your customer's cost of production. Inasmuch as the cost of production plays an important part in determining the profits of an industry, the various factors entering into it must be examined with great care in order to determine whether total costs will increase or decrease during the period under study.

Prices also are important for practically the same reason, as we have seen. Prices respond to changes in basic business conditions differently, however, in the case of industries where free competition is the rule than they do in the case of industries more or less under the control of some strong interest constituting a monopoly. If competition is present, prices will freely respond to changes in the business trend and to changes in the average price of all commodities. If, however, the industry is a practical monopoly, prices may be held under such complete control that changes in the business trend and in the price of other commodities may find very little reflection in the price of the industry's product.

We must not forget that the labor situation may affect future producing activity, not only through wage changes, but also through troubles resulting in strikes and boycotts. Therefore, the character of the labor used in the industry, the extent to which it is organized, the nature of any existing agreements, and the general relations of employers and employees should be ascertained. The probability of labor troubles in other industries, especially fuel and transportation, should be estimated.

The condition of the money market should be determined with the idea of forming a judgment as to the future course of money rates. Increasing money rates mean increased interest charges and cost of working capital, while a decrease in money rates means the contrary.

The probability of tariff changes should be considered. Increased tariff rates on the product of the industry will tend to curtail imports and enable domestic manufacturers to maintain prices on a higher basis than if the importation of the product were unrestricted by import duties.

The crop situation has a bearing on the future
activity of most industries, because the farmer buys
approximately 30 per cent. of all the manufactured
products produced. When good crops are market-
able at profitable prices, farmers buy freely, and
there is generally a good demand for most manufactured goods. When crops are poor and prices
are low compared with the prices of the things the
farmer buys, he curtails his purchasing, and the
effect is immediately felt in the manufacturing industries. Hence, the outlook for crops and the
price of farm products are important items to
determine.

An eye should also be kept on the progress of
legislation at Washington. This may take the form
of tariff or price-fixing discussions, or matters relat-
ing to the labor situation. Despite the slogan of
less government in business, we must recognize that
there will always be considerable government in
business.

By following the above general rules you will be
able to obtain a fairly good opinion as to the probable purchasing attitude of your customers in each
industry.

Having obtained a knowledge of conditions,
present and future, or the industries to which you
wish to sell, you are in a position to plan your sales
and advertising campaigns to fit your customer's
needs. You have time to prepare for increased activity and can be on hand with the goods when they

are needed. If your sales field embraces more than one line of activity, you can shift as conditions change to keep your efforts concentrated on your best market.

When the outlook is unfavorable and an industry is to go through a temporary decline, your studies will warn you in time. Your credit department has an opportunity to get cleaned up before things get too tight, and your sales manager can avoid waste of time and money on a barren field.

And by selling as described above, you can base your decision on a full and complete knowledge of conditions as they are and will exist, you will avoid risk, worry, and loss — in fact, make the most of every opportunity. It is hardly necessary to add that it will enable you to reduce the margin of error in your business judgment score to a negligible fraction, thereby materially increasing both your sales and your net profit.

Chapter XII

THE TREND OF BUSINESS

SIMPLIFICATION and proper distribution are America's great business needs. During the last twenty years or more, efficiency in manufacturing processes has been the outstanding development in the business world. Anything that would increase the efficiency of workers has been eagerly seized upon. Variations in methods of payment have been tried. These range all the way from the making of detailed studies of the time required to complete each separate operation in a manufacturing process to methods of profit-sharing whereby the worker earns, not only his pay, but also a share in the total profits of the company. Most careful scrutiny has been exercised in reducing the time required to do an operation, workers being instructed how to hold their hands, how to stand, how many motions to make, for example, in putting the soles on a pair of shoes. In the up-to-date plant to-day, some form of all these various efficiency-promoting schemes may be found.

The efficiency so noticeable in production is, however, almost completely lacking in distribution. From the time a finished product leaves the manufacturer's hand to the time it reaches the ultimate consumer, the manufacturer's selling price has, in a great majority of cases, been doubled and tripled, on account of the cost of passing it through a number of intermediate hands, and the profits which each middleman feels to be his due.

For example, a cotton shirtwaist was bought in a Chicago clothing store for $6.95. It was taken to a jewelry store, weighed, and found to tip the scales at six ounces. Its six ounces at an average price for cotton would cost approximately 5 to 10 cents. One reason for the spread between the cost of the raw material and the price of the finished product is without question the fact that women all want different shirtwaists. There is lack of simplification. Sugar and a drop of peppermint make peppermints selling for 50 cents a pound — yet in New York sugar sells at an average price around 5 to 6 cents a pound. This is another case where efficiency in manufacture is overwhelmed by inefficiency in distribution.

You may say that the retailer is making an enormous profit on these articles. The probabilities are that the stores do not make even a fair profit, during many phases of the business cycle, nor does the maker or distributor. The trouble lies in the system. That the system can be changed is evident when we consider the match industry. Our lowest monetary unit, the cent, will purchase a box of matches. Matches at a cent a box represent efficiency both in production and marketing. American manufacturers are competing, at a cent a box, with the Swedish and Japanese match makers.

The match represents the value of simplification in manufacture and distribution. Machinery and system both in the shop and in the market result in the cent-a-box match. There is the wood in the match and in the box. There is the chemical compound in the match and on two sides of the box — the safety kind. There is some printing also. Taking the match and its container, the manufacturer, the jobber, the distributor, and the retailer, we have an operation which makes us wonder that we get matches for a cent a box. There is an efficient system back of the match.

During the coming twenty years, the present inefficiency or lack of proper marketing methods will tend to be eliminated. Just as concentrated attention toward the goal of manufacturing efficiency has brought results during the past, so will concentrated attention toward simplification and efficient distribution bring results during the coming years.

In the working out of this simplification we shall witness a continued development of chain stores. They are having a tremendous run to-day. They are springing up like weeds in every community. Local merchants are beginning to become panic stricken. They fear that the chain store is to swallow up everything. Grocers, druggists, and clothiers are especially troubled. Altogether there are over a million small merchants in America who are vitally affected by this development. There is no sign of slackening in it for several years to come.

The chain store is efficiently organized and prospers for that reason. If the local merchant will adopt the same up-to-date methods of economical merchandising, he need have nothing to fear from chain store competition. However, the chain store will encounter the same obstacle that has interfered with efficiency and service on the railroads and in manufacture in our various industries; namely, labor unionization.

Chain stores will have their troubles just as the railroads and manufacturers have had theirs. The unionization of labor has tended to raise the cost of doing business in both transportation and manufacturing lines. The employees of chain stores have not as yet become unionized. They are hard workers and give full service for the wages they receive. The day will come when they will be unionized. Clerks, truck drivers, and buyers will organize and become as independent as the typical plumber is to-day. That day will mean the end of the phenomenal progress which chain stores are achieving. Then the chain store sales will drop off, operating expenses will increase, and they will have to adopt a more modern form of merchandising or give way to a new order. Distributors by chain store methods should realize that labor is the weak spot in their armor.

Closely allied with the future of the chain store is the future of the self-help store. This is not a new idea. In the self-help store, the customer enters at one door, proceeds along a definitely planned path around the counters, and thence out an exit door. He is expected, during the course of this passage, to help himself to the goods he desires and pay for them just before leaving at the exit. The self-help system eliminates labor difficulty to a considerable extent and enables a store to give excellent service at low cost. The saving compared with the ordinary cost of serving a customer in the average retail shop is large.

The self-help idea is applicable to all kinds of stores — book stores, drug stores, grocery stores, five and ten-cent stores, and such like. It is true that the average merchant cannot get the advantage of collective buying unless he himself joins a chain. Any merchant, however, can install a self-help system of selling independently. This, of course, means more than reorganizing the fixtures of his store. He must change his entire attitude. The self-help stores, for instance, are very dependent upon advertising; much more so than are the chain stores and local merchants. The latter must advertise more than ever when he adopts the self-help system.

If the local merchant continues as at present, he will be eliminated from American business to make way for more modern machinery of distribution.

The self-help store is a step along the line mentioned in the previous part of this chapter wherein efficiency in distribution was pointed out to be the goal toward which business men would strive during the coming years.

The self-help idea is analogous to the pay-as-you enter street car. The idea is one that will be developed in a great many ways and, in so far as the distribution of goods is concerned, it may be expected to be developed enormously during coming years. This does not mean, of course, that high-grade stores, catering to people who wish to telephone their orders and have their goods delivered, are going out of business. These stores have been developed to a great degree and will continue to function and serve the people who wish that kind of service. The big development will be in connection with the self-help idea.

During the course of the coming years more stress will be laid on developing the efficiency of buyers in contrast to the efficiency of salesmen. Heretofore, salesmanship has been the outstanding point in transactions involving the exchange of goods. Huge salaries have been paid to exceptionally good salesmen. While buyers have been in some cases well paid, generally speaking they have not been on such a high basis as salesmen. Salesmen are frequently placed on a commission basis and are spurred on by all kinds of inducements to increase their sales. Buyers but infrequently have any reward coming to them as a result of efficiency in buying, over and beyond their salaries. Yet a moment's thought will show that the buyer is just as important in any transaction as the seller. Buyers are not always enabled to sit back and wait for the seller to come to them. They must frequently go into the market and cover their needs at whatever prices they can obtain. This is especially true in the case of manufacturers whose producing activities must be maintained.

Frequently, there is a situation wherein all but one or two of the materials necessary to continue production are available. It is then necessary to obtain the missing materials immediately in order not to block operations. An efficient buyer under such circumstances may be able to save his concern considerable money by intelligent work. Generally speaking, therefore, we look for more emphasis to be laid on efficient buying during the coming years than has been the case heretofore. One reason for the existence of the present high-priced salesman is the inefficiency of the present buyer.

There will probably be increased demand for trade association activity. In many competitive lines, individual manufacturers are finding that, instead of competition being the life of trade, it is frequently its death. Individual producers are given to proceeding in the dark because they do not know what other manufacturers in their line are doing. They have no way of knowing how the supply of their product compares with the demand for it. They cannot adjust their producing activity to the conditions of the market. As a result, there are frequently periods of serious over-production and, conversely, periods in which stocks are very light and the better informed manufacturers reap a harvest because others have sized up the situation incorrectly.

The gathering of manufacturers and jobbers into trade associations keeps the various manufacturers informed regarding the activities of their industry, the best methods of producing and selling their product, and the general business policies that should be followed from time to time in the management of their concerns. In other words, by making greater use of trade associations, the future will be a period of greater co-operation among manufacturers and jobbers than it has been heretofore when cut-throat competition was largely the rule.

Along with the formation of trade associations in various lines of industry and business, there will naturally arise an increasing demand for statistics covering production, sales, prices, costs, etc. These will become available because it will be by means of them that an association will keep its members informed of conditions in its own and related lines.

Another development that is in prospect is the business counselor or commissioner. For the same reason that certain cities have done away with mayors and boards of aldermen and placed their affairs in the hands of a business administrator on a salary basis, the various industries will place their affairs in the hands of a commissioner who will so organize the affairs of the industry as to bring the greatest amount of profit to the concerns in that industry. The commissioner now at the head of the moving picture industry is an example of this probability. The appointment of a federal judge as high commissioner of baseball is another example.

The coming twenty-five years should see a resumption of the constructive activities of so-called "captains" of industry. The meaning will be clear when we consider that the period of 1875 to 1900 was a period in which great fortunes were established by industries conceived and developed by men who started comparatively poor and unknown and finally emerged as leaders in the business world. They were really captains of industry and their wealth might be termed constructive wealth. During the period between 1900 and 1925, however, the outstanding figures in the business and financial world were speculators. Roosevelt characterized their wealth as predatory wealth, in contrast to constructive wealth. Of course, there were a few outstanding exceptions in the last twenty years but the majority of the prominent figures were speculators. During the coming twenty years, however, business men of the type of Carnegie and Hill will again come to the fore. The foundation of their industries will be *service* and *efficiency*.

Chapter XIII

FINANCIAL INDEPENDENCE

A FEW years ago an investigation and study was made of the financial experience of the average man.[1] It shows his position at various ages and reveals a condition that demands a remedy.

If we begin with one hundred average men we find them entering the business world between the ages of sixteen and twenty-four, depending on how much time they spend in school. The ten years between twenty and thirty should really be charged to education. During this period a job should be worth what it teaches and not what it pays. It is safe to assume that any money earned over and above the amount necessary to pay living expenses is spent along educational lines. Correspondence courses, night classes, and good books constitute a most profitable investment at this particular point in a man's career. We can assume then that our average individual reaches thirty ,with a reasonable

[1] The figures in this survey have been questioned because they do not check exactly with the mortality tables of the great life insurance companies. A thorough investigation, however, discloses the fact that the estimates on financial conditions are reliable. They are an underestimate of the facts rather than an overestimate.

education and some valuable experience in at least one line of work.

At *thirty-five* we begin to see a decided change. *Five out of our hundred men have died, ten out of the hundred have become wealthy, ten more are in good circumstances and are considered well-to-do, forty are in moderate circumstances, are earning a*

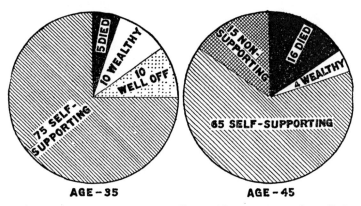

Age 35, 10 wealthy, 10 well off, 75 self-supporting, 5 have died.
Age 45, 4 wealthy, 65 self-supporting, 15 non-supporting, 16 have died.

living for themselves and families — they seem to be getting on. The remaining thirty-five have shown no improvement in their condition. They are holding their jobs and earning the salary of the average man ten years their junior.

At *forty-five* eleven more have died — sixteen in all. Only four of the hundred that started twenty-five years before are wealthy. These are four of the ten who were wealthy at thirty-five; the other six have lost their money.

The ten who were in good circumstances at thirty-five are now classified with the sixty-five who are still working and are self-supporting but who have no resources outside of their regular salary or wage. Fifteen men out of our hundred are no longer self-

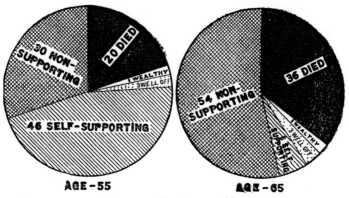

Age 55, 1 wealthy, 3 well off, 46 self-supporting, 30 non-supporting, 20 have died.

Age 65, 1 wealthy, 3 well off, 6 self-supporting, 54 non-supporting, 36 have died.

supporting owing to illness, accident, or other circumstance. A few of them are still earning something, but not enough to support themselves.

At *fifty-five* only eighty of our men remain — twenty have died. One of the four who was wealthy at forty-five has become very rich. Two of the four are still in good circumstances, but the other has lost everything. One of the sixty-five who was working and depended upon his salary at the age of forty-five, has become wealthy. This gives us three in good circumstances at the age of fifty-five. Forty-six are still working for their living without any accumulation. Thirty are more or less dependent upon their children, their relations, or upon charity for support.

At *sixty-five* we witness the last act of the tragedy. Thirty-six of our hundred representative American men are dead, one is still rich, three are wealthy, six are still at work and self-supporting, fifty-four, or over half of them, are dependent upon children or relations and charity.

The real tragedy of this deplorable situation however, is revealed by the fact that *ninety of these hundred men made enough money between thirty and fifty to keep themselves and their families in comparative luxury for the rest of their lives.*

Analysis shows that our school system is partly to blame. The average man spends eight years in grammar school and then may add four years in high school. A few continue and add four more in college or university. All of this time is spent in learning things which may be helpful in the making of money. Not one-half hour is spent in teaching the student what to do with the money after he gets it; and there is very little sense in spending the best part of one's life in working hard to get a few dollars if those dollars do not earn for you after you get them.

Coming out of school, the average American boy goes to work with a vengeance. He is ambitious, he works hard, he learns rapidly, and is soon able to produce more than he actually needs for his own living expenses. Sooner or later he finds himself with a few dollars to spare, a few dollars that are available for investments. In nine cases out of ten he either lets this money around where it earns nothing for him or "invests" it in some promotion — oil well, gold mine, egg preservers, paper milk bottle, or wireless telephone wire — it makes little difference which. He loses it all. And so it goes. For the next twenty-five or thirty years he makes much money, saves some of it quite by accident, and loses by far the larger portion of what he saves.

If you are to avoid this same tragic experience, you must employ fundamental principles in the handling of your surplus funds exactly as you do in the conduct of your business. If you will take the trouble to study and follow the few principles outlined in the remainder of this chapter and in the next two, you will have a definite and scientific plan that will carry you to financial independence exactly as any well-marked highway will carry you to the city at its terminus.

Obviously, we must first have a fund before we can do any investing. In most cases that fund must be accumulated by saving a part of the money that is earned. Right here the average man makes his first mistake; he does not save systematically and therefore saves about one-half to one-tenth as much as he should. If he tried to run his business in the way he finances his home — without any definite plan — he would end in bankruptcy inside of a year. Home expenses should be budgeted. Intelligent planning in advance will enable you to live just as well as you do now and with much less expense.

It is possible that there is more fun in saving than in spending. We shall solve the saving problem by employing this very principle. Saving is no trick at all when you have learned how to " spend money at your bank." You will never get anywhere if you try to save " what is left," but if you will make up your mind to a definite amount that can be put into the bank each month and then put it there, first thing, before you pay the rent or anything else, you will find your bank account growing at a very satisfactory rate.

The following table, which was made up from the Manning budget and subsequent study made by my associates gives you an outline average for various sized incomes. Please bear in mind that the expenditures noted are maximum and that the savings noted are minimum. You will probably be able to make a better showing than the figure indicated.

One's first savings should be used for life insurance; but insure for protection rather than as an investment. Buy protection with your in-

TYPICAL BUDGETS FOR VARIOUS INCOMES
FOR AN AVERAGE AMERICAN FAMILY — TWO ADULTS AND TWO CHILDREN

Income	Necessities (Per month)					Duties (Per month)			Surplus (Insurance and Inc. Tax not deducted)		
Per year	Per cent.	Food	Shelter	Clothes	Operating maintenance	Per cent.	Education, Recreation, etc.	Benevolence	Per cent	Per month	Per year
$ 2,500.00	71.2	$ 50.00	$ 45.00	$ 27.00	$ 26.33	19.2	$ 20.00	$ 20.00	9.6	$ 20.00	$ 240.00
3,000.00	66.0	55.00	50.00	30.00	30.00	20.0	25.00	25.00	14.0	35.00	420.00
3,500.00	64.0	60.00	57.00	34.00	35.67	20.6	30.00	30.00	15.4	45.00	540.00
4,000.00	61.2	65.00	60.00	38.00	41.00	22.3	41.00	33.33	16.5	55.00	660.00
5,000.00	58.8	70.00	70.00	45.00	65.00	21.7	48.75	41.67	19.5	81.25	975.00
7,500.00	48.0	80.00	90.00	60.00	70.00	24.4	87.50	62.50	28.0	175.00	2,100.00
10,000.00	43.0	85.00	110.00	68.00	95.00	25.0	125.00	83.33	32.0	267.00	3,204.00
12,500.00	36.5	90.00	115.00	75.00	100.00	22.7	132.50	104.17	40.8	425.00	5,100.00
15,000.00	32.8	95.00	125.00	80.00	110.00	21.2	140.00	125.00	46.0	575.00	6,900.00
20,000.00	28.1	108.00	135.00	100.00	125.00	22.4	207.00	166.67	49.5	825.00	9,900.00
25,000.00	26.4	125.00	150.00	125.00	150.00	23.0	283.33	208.33	50.0	1041.67	12,500.00
30,000.00	25.0	140.00	175.00	135.00	175.00	25.0	375.00	250.00	50.0	1250.00	15,000.00
40,000.00	22.5	150.00	200.00	150.00	250.00	23.5	450.00	333.33	54.0	1800.00	21,600.00
50,000.00	21.6	175.00	250.00	175.00	300.00	42.4	600.00	416.67	54.0	2250.00	27,000.00

surance fund. The remainder, or your surplus, may next be divided into two distinct funds — one an investment fund and the second a speculative fund.

The investment fund is to be placed in securities that will bring in a regular income each year. The speculative fund is to be used to purchase certain securities which you expect to sell later at a profit. Broadly speaking, the investment fund should be used in the purchase of stable bonds, the speculative fund for your common stocks. If your income is $5000 or under, it is possible that all your savings for some time should be used as an investment fund. Speculation should be attempted only by a man who does not need the additional income and can afford to wait from a year to three years for his profits.

CHAPTER XIV

INVESTING YOUR INCOME

THE moment your savings account has reached the $1,000 mark you are ready to begin enjoying two incomes, one from your work and one from your investments.

You are ready to start the selection of bonds that will provide you with a steady and comfortable income during your declining years. If you are purchasing in any quantity it may be well to deal through a regular broker. Select one who is well known, of excellent reputation and a member of one of the large stock exchanges. For smaller purchases, deal through some conservative and reliable bond house or place your order directly with your own banker who will purchase for you any bonds you may want.

What then are the fundamental principles by which to select your investments?

First, *security*.

Since you are lending capital to obtain income, you should be satisfied both that there is property in form that cannot be dissipated or transferred without record, and that your money is to be applied in some way that is reproductive. That is, it does not satisfy you, as an investor, when you know that the borrowed money is going only to pay current bills or bank loans, or make good losses that may have impaired capital beyond remedy.

The security afforded by mortgage is a matter of degree, expressed under general headings such as:

First Mortgage,
Refunding, or First & Refunding Mortgage,
General, or General & Refunding,
Collateral, or First Lien & Collateral.

Except as the term " first mortgage " is used by itself, it may imply much or little in regard to security. The matter must be examined in each case. I have recommended recently a first and refunding bond which has a first mortgage on a new part of the property that I would rather take than any under the original mortgage.

The term " general mortgage " has largely supplanted the earlier and franker admission of second or third mortgage.

The word " collateral," whether by itself or as first lien and collateral, puts you on notice immediately for further inquiry. Where the collateral deposited as security for your bonds is wholly stocks, your position has slight advantage over direct stock ownership.

Convertible bonds may, or may not, have an interest in mortgages on the property. The better convertible issues, of which the number is limited, serve a very satisfactory purpose at certain phases in the market when they can be bought practically on their investment basis.

The term " debenture " signifies an issue without mortgage; that is, a note. In event of any difficulty this stands no better than bank loans and other bills payable. It has become the custom to surround debentures with certain restrictive covenants which have had varying degrees of success. Usually, however, if a waiver of rights is necessary to save a financial life, it is possible to obtain the required consents.

Second, *marketability*.

It is not indispensable that your bond be listed on one of the stock exchanges, but this is of great assistance in keeping track of your investment. It is necessary that the issue you hold be of sufficient volume and importance to have an established level of buying and selling among dealers at some of the important centers. The existence of such a market in absence of listing is especially notable in the case of municipal bonds. One has no trouble in learning instantly the value of obligations of any of our larger cities. Contrary to the impression of some persons, the lower you go in the grade of bond, the more essential it is to have quick and ready marketability. The danger is that, even should you have warning of impending change in the condition of the property, you could find no means of selling an unknown issue.

Third, *yield*.

Income, of course, implies that there must be confidence in earning power. The term yield, as applied to bonds, is simple. Consider a 4 per cent. bond for $1,000 payable in ten years. At what price must it be purchased to yield a net return of 6 per cent.? At this required rate of 6 per cent., compounded semi-annually, the present value of $1,000 payable ten years from now is $553.67. At the same rate, the present value of the twenty semi-annual interest installments of $20 each, payable at successive dates, is $297.53. The required price, therefore, is the sum of the foregoing present values of principal and interest, or $851.20. It is rarely necessary, however, for the investor to compute prices and net returns, as there are available convenient tables of bond values giving the desired information at a glance.

Fourth, *ethical factors*.

Besides the three items, generally identified with bonds, there is another group of considerations that seems to me as important as any. There certainly are good and bad businesses. The process of the years is unmistakably working to a higher moral tone in our business affairs. Neglect of this was costly to some holders of distillery and brewery securities.

Fair treatment of the public, of employees, of those who supply raw materials and those who distribute the manufactured product, on the part of an industry, augurs a much more prosperous future than any " public-be-damned " attitude.

There is discoverable a fundamental trend in any given group. For example, the chart of total sales per year, compared with gross earnings per year, of certain large power companies shows a very steady trend to a decreasing unit price for the output sold. Where this has been accomplished without a compensating drop in net, it shows increased efficiency. This is one of the best grounds for confidence.

As many of you know, in relation to railroads, the " operating ratio " is studied from month to month as revealing the story of improved or declining fortunes.

In the industrial field generally, it is not to be denied that a rather disturbing problem is presented by the tendency to increasing overhead. There are many examples to indicate that there is distinctly a limit to efficiency in large organizations.

Bonds, because of their standard denominations and ready negotiability, have become the typical investment. There is a bond market, just as there is a market for the commodities which sustain life or clothe or house us and for the stock certificates which represent a share in the supply of them. These commodities tend to a price movement directly with the business trend, being worth more in " good times " and less in " bad times " in accordance with the effective demand — that is, the ability of the public to gratify its desires. Bonds, however, are contracts for fixed payments in money. They are sold highest when, because of restricted business, current funds command lowest interest rates. On the other hand, a steady decline in bond prices follows high interest rates due to a shortage of money for financing. Over-expansion is a sure sign of the coming of depression.

Let me state a concrete example. Most bonds are selling to-day at prices higher than since 1917. But after 1917 there followed three years of the sharpest drop the bond market had seen since the Civil War. Should you, therefore, sell bonds now? Turn to your statistics of business and study fundamental conditions. In 1917 we were in the early stage of the greatest area of inflation — or " good times " — ever recorded. This was closed in 1920, just when bonds sold lowest.

Shall you, then, sell your long-term bonds during the next " boom " ?

What has been said thus far has had reference to the business trend. There is still a further factor to consider on bonds — the long-swing trend of interest rates. This, too, bears out the law of action and reaction. From each peak, in our experience, represented by an investment level of 7 to 8 per cent., there has been a general trend downward for twenty to twenty-five years, to half the rate or less, followed by an upward trend for a nearly equal period to the next peak. What the cause may be — whether the slower movement of fixed capital than commodities, or the wastes of great wars with which interest peaks coincide; or whether the old maxim " shirtsleeves to shirtsleeves in three generations " is expressive of wastefulness and moral breakdown that underlie both wars and interest rates, I'll not here attempt to say. But the fact is a fundamental for investors. It is responsible for what is sometimes called the major bond swing.

In 1920, we closed such a period with the yield on investment issues at a high point not recorded since 1875. What has happened since 1920 indicates that we are now in a new phase. Both on current money rates and bond yields we are retracing, almost step by step, the old chart of reconstruction days. We are doing this despite factors in the situation that are dissimilar, such as our change from a debtor and borrowing, to a creditor and lending nation. A reason for the turn in bond yields at the level of 1875 is, doubtless, the fact that we escaped the fiat money basis of 1873 because we had such an improved credit position. Through such escape we avoided the extraordinary yields of that year — upwards of 8 per cent. compared with 6.72 per cent. in 1920. From the present status of the bond market, I expect to see 3½ per cent., or less, as the standard investment return before any one can buy on a 7 per cent. basis bonds of the high grade obtainable during the post-war inflation.

The relation of the shorter business phase and the major trend in money rates is that of the ocean

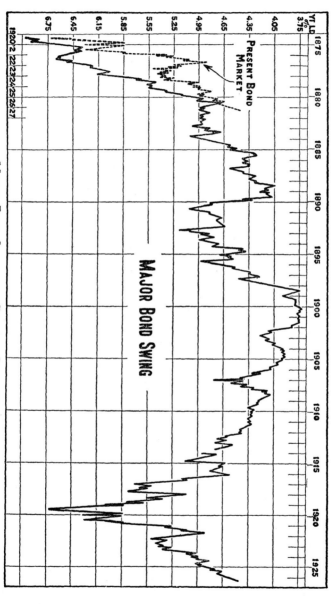

MAJOR BOND SWING AND PRESENT BOND MARKET

waves and the tides. No navigator is safe without
reckoning them. He is the skillful mariner who
knows how to take advantage of both. Before he
will venture from port the sailor judges his craft
for seaworthiness. Storms will come. He must,
at times, be working against wind and wave and tide
as well. He bases his judgment on statistics. Ton-
nage, draught, beam, and engine power are considered in the light of conditions at sea experienced

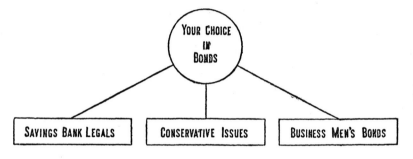

over a term of years. What will do for one voyage
will not do for another. Above all, he invariably
demands a " margin of safety." Very similar principles apply in the use of statistics for the testing
of bonds.

Certain requirements laid down by law, the accumulation of years, restrict the investment of savings bank and trust funds in the several states. The
law assumes a high degree of inertia about these
funds. Purchases are made by vote of a committee
whose opinion, once formed, is not easily reversed.

It not infrequently happens that the bonds are held to maturity. Under such circumstances security is the prime essential. Interest return and yield can be accorded only secondary consideration.

Next in order comes a large investment group classed as conservative bonds, satisfactory for the bulk of corporation or private investment funds. These, aside from governments or municipals, are issues secured by mortgage, with ample equity, on the property of railroad, utility, or industrial corporations that can show a satisfactory business record. It rarely is possible to admit to such lists a wholly new issue. Preference is given to bonds which have been outstanding for a term of years so that they have " seasoned." Furthermore, such issues can be examined for their record of marketability, or resale value.

All other bonds which are worth considering for investment come under the general designation of business men's issues. There is a wide difference in merit. A certain percentage selected from such a list may be taken in connection with the proper amount of conservative issues for any person's own funds. The more issues over which this part of a fund is distributed and the more restrained one is in selecting the higher yields, the larger percentage of his fund may be so employed. The investor must watch the effect of changing business conditions and be willing to sell on notice.

The element which accounts for any one of these

bonds continuing to sell apparently out of line with the general market may be either —

(*a*) Lack of first grade security in its claim against property. This factor, offset by a long record of ample earnings and the faithful payment of interest, may still make it attractive for some buyers.

(*b*) Weak earnings record, where the security is a first claim on property of great value, present or prospective. In this situation, the buyer may sometimes be warranted in taking a bond even despite the possibility of a receivership. Usually, in this case, no advantage is lost by waiting until the worst has actually happened.

The best business man's purchase is a bond that has come through a drastic reorganization.

Diversification is one of the fundamental principles of investment that never may be ignored. No matter how strong the security, or how attractive, one never should deviate from the policy of distributing his funds over a list rather than concentrating in one or a few issues. Distribution is best accomplished by adopting a regular unit of purchase, say one, three, or five bonds. The law of averages thus is applied to any element of risk. No benefit is gained by " averaging " the *price* of your holdings. This leads to doubling up in those things which have proved your poorest selections rather than the best.

Neither is it good policy to buy two or more different issues in the same company.

I am often asked by some of my clients to advise for them a list of what they term speculative bonds. In most cases the speculative element is the only certainty about it. Putting this in the form of a bond or note is only a sugar coating which serves to induce the purchaser to stake more of his capital and start his risk from a higher price level than he would consider if offered stock. There are, occasionally, speculative possibilities in defaulted bonds, either government obligations, direct or guaranteed, or such corporation issues as have some real assets behind them. But it is much easier, with any ordinary amount of capital, to distribute your risk by the purchase of common stocks of sound corporations enjoying a listed regular market.

Again I say, it is fundamental to success to distinguish clearly between the commitments you make for speculative profit and the funds you *invest for income*. If you make the right choice of bonds and buy them at the right periods you will have, from time to time, a very substantial increase in your principal. But when you begin to pay more heed to this increase than to the security of income, you have started on the road to paying simply a high price for a poor speculation.

The financing of proposed construction, especially for a new concern, is extra hazardous. It should not be considered unless by one of means sufficient to back up his original commitment in case estimates go wrong. Too often the best laid plans fail on some miscalculation. This was the condition revealed in the ten-word telegraphic report of one engineer's investigation:

" Fine dam by mill-site — no mill by dam-site."

I have before me the facts of a very recent case where conditions leading to a receivership were most puzzling. The location, industry and market seemed excellent. Construction and equipment were rated the best. Operations, for a period of months, showed a margin over cost, but disappointingly small as compared with capital charges. A bondholders' protective committee has discovered that the plant never was equipped to run the entire process upon which estimates were based. Lack of $150,000 to complete equipment, after many millions had been spent, throttled operations. The backers of the enterprise had twice been to the banks and investors to sell bonds and apparently dared not test out confidence by returning with an admission that the estimates had been again exceeded.

It is in order, here, to comment on a totally different type of security, in favor with some investors — preferred stocks. I earnestly indorse the statement of one of Boston's best known investment bankers that " preferred stocks are a very much overrated type of security." Preferred stocks are not, as some have been misled to believe, the equivalent of bonds without maturity. They cannot. legally, set up any obligation except for income, if earned, or assets in liquidation, *after all debts,* including bonds and notes, have been paid. Restrictions, sinking funds, and other frills are waived invariably when need arises. The preferred stockholder is rather in the position of a silent partner, limited as to share in profits and without voice, under ordinary conditions, in management. I do not mean that no preferred stocks are admissible holdings. I do mean that a selection entirely, or in large part, of preferred stocks is not an investment list.

The preferreds are popular in a few states where old tax laws lay a heavy burden on the conscientious owner of bonds. These states are well-known and names of investors living therein are eagerly sought for what the Street calls "sucker lists." To the victims of the "tax-exempt preferred" promoters my advice is that you get together and demand reformation of your tax laws.

Having determined *what* to buy, there is then presented for the investor the question *when* to buy it, and when to sell. Let me put it by example.

A man who sold out his business, retiring with $100,000 in 1901, used the very best judgment and selected issues like Lake Shore 3½'s, Illinois Central 3½'s, and General Electric 3½'s, all around 101. At that time he was content with $3500 a year for his living. From that day to the present, there never has been the slightest question about the security of the issues in which he invested. Nevertheless, **in**

1920 his principal had shrunk to $60,000 and with his income he could buy only a $1,750 living. Another man, starting the same way, read the signs of the money market and began to make exchanges out of his old bonds, keeping up with the increase of return. In 1913 to 1917, he accomplished complete switching over into short-term notes with the high-coupon rates. As a result, he maintained his capital fund at $100,000 and arrived in 1920 with an income of $7,000. Then, following the reversal trend of money conditions, he immediately changed his holdings into old 4 and 5 per cent. bonds, selling at great discounts, which would give him, for an average of twenty years, an income of $7,500 a year. That man to-day has more than double the buying power of the other. His principal, instead of being around $100,000, could be marketed for $125,000. It is these advantages which are obtained by careful study of the investment situation.

FINANCIAL INDEPENDENCE

The road to financial independence lies open for any one who will save systematically and invest intelligently. Only a fortunate few can expect *sudden* acquisition of such a sum as will provide release from money-cares, present and future. Over the period of ordinary earning power, however, most men should be able to build an income fund reasonably commen-

surate with average annual earning power. Con-
sistent saving and investment can be helped by a
definite, carefully worked out program, inspired by
assurance of ultimate financial independence.

Unfortunately the desire to save for future independence meets strong resistance in the desire to
spend for present enjoyment. To combat this desire, it is well to see just what length of time is necessary, with varying amounts saved, to reach the desired
goal. A study of the extraordinary power of compound interest should furnish adequate inspiration
to the man having any real ambition to build an investment fund for old age independence.

The accompanying chart [How Money Grows At
Compound Interest] indicates the growth of money
compounded semi-annually at 4 per cent., 5 per cent.
and 6 per cent. It assumes a starting point of $10,000.
Multiples or divisors can be used to indicate growth
possible from any definite amount which may be available. The original sum can be invested in good bonds
to-day to yield better than 5 per cent. Then it becomes necessary to invest the income from semi-
annual coupons at the same rate, and to keep all funds
working constantly.

Every dollar saved to-day means that the fulfill-
ment of present desires is postponed or canceled in
favor of future desires or needs. The $2,000 which
is saved to-day, instead of being used to purchase
some luxury, will provide $100 a year income for
the rest of one's life. Moreover, if, as I believe, the

general trend of commodity prices is downward, the purchasing power of both capital and income should be greater ten or fifteen years hence than it is to-day.

It is only by considering accumulation as a definite charge against monthly income that conscientious saving is possible. It is not essential, but certainly advisable, that definite arrangements be made to lay aside specific amounts at stated intervals. To do this it is almost necessary to systematize expenditures. In other words, expenses should be so budgeted in relation to income as to provide a surplus which can be turned to investment purposes.

For younger men especially, there should be inspiration in studying figures that show what can be done through regular saving and investment. Others may well consider the following compilation as providing a lesson in thrift for their sons. Again invoking the power of compound interest, it is clear that moderate monthly saving, if started early in life, offers financial independence at old age.

The tabulation below shows results for monthly deposits of $10, $25, and $50 respectively. Consider the $10 column. At 5 per cent., the interest rate assumed throughout, a $10 monthly deposit compounded semi-annually would become $2,000 in a little more than twelve years. I have used the definite period, twelve and one-half years, in this table. When the round sum of $2,000 is reached, it is invested at 5 per cent. and continues to grow simply through interest accretions while the monthly deposit is working upward toward another $2,000. The various sums used obviously can be multiplied or divided as greater or less amounts are available for deposit.

How Money Grows At 5 Per Cent. Compound Interest When Regular Monthly Deposits Are Made

At age 25	$10	$25	$50
	saved monthly becomes		
At age 37½ ..	$2,000	$5,000	$10,000
	which, reinvested, becomes		
At age 50 ...	3,707	9,269	18,539
	and meanwhile monthly deposits have created another		
	2,000	5,000	10,000
a total of	$5,707	$14,269	$28,539
	which, reinvested, becomes		
At age 62½ ..	10,580	26,453	52,909
	While monthly deposits have again reached		
	2,000	5,000	10,000
a total of	$12,580	$31,453	$62,909
	which, reinvested, becomes		
At age 75 ...	23,322	58,311	116,629
	While monthly deposits have again reached		
	2,000	5,000	10,000
a total of	$25,322	$63,311	$126,629

It should be recognized that there are certain differences between the theory of a tabulation such as this and its practical application. The same is true of the method proposed by the accompanying graph. In both cases, it is assumed that each dollar of income is reinvested immediately as it becomes available. As a practical matter, there are distinct difficulties in attaining such an end.

Over a period of years it will often be found impossible to reinvest to advantage certain small and uneven amounts. In some instances the return received will be somewhat larger than that assumed for the entire investment. In other cases it will be smaller. To the extent that various influences bring about a change from the definite figures set down, it is, of course, obvious that some change will be noted in the results.

In either of these plans for building a retirement fund, security should be emphasized strongly and good bonds should take very much the largest proportion of the funds. At times, however, the investor will be warranted in turning a portion of his investment into stocks. This should be done only as the fund becomes large enough to permit broad diversification. Moreover, there should be no attempt to increase capital in this way except where it can be done at minimum risk. Many opportunities will appear during the life of the funds to buy good dividend-paying stocks with every assurance of substantial profit. Only the best of common stocks should be purchased and then only when clear that a real opportunity exists. Naturally non-dividend paying issues should not be considered.

Both methods are based on security of capital and growth through moderate but regular income. Any divergence from the original policy of emphasizing security should be avoided. There is no need for haste or for taking undue risk. These results can be accomplished without it.

Among the recollections of my boyhood, the outstanding impression is that many men down in Gloucester retired from active business life at what would now seem an early age. Some of you can recall how in those days there were plenty of men from fifty to sixty who seemed to live in relative luxury on their incomes. These were the men, as far as I know the circumstances, who took their accumulation of money and put it into investments back in 1860-1875, just at the beginning of the last upswing or reconstructive phase in the bond swing. Yields of 7 per cent. were frequent in those days and incomes were much smaller than would be adequate now. Twenty-five thousand dollars was sufficient and fifty thousand was a fortune.

You can start your investment fund with assurance that you will have increasing bond prices, which will add to every dollar you save, as well as compound interest which alone would double your fund every dozen years. Work out a plan that suits your particular circumstances and begin building that " other income " to-day.

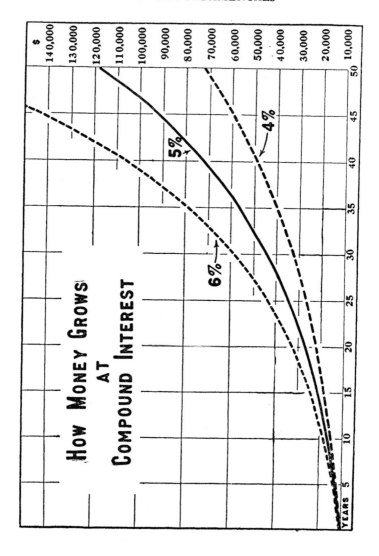

How Money Grows at Compound Interest

Chapter XV

SUCCESSFUL SPECULATION

IF possible, I should like to clear up the more or less popular conception that speculation is gambling and that the man who buys and sells speculative stocks is a gambler.

This, of course, is not true if the man who is speculating is doing so intelligently. In this case it is not only a perfectly legitimate and profitable pursuit, but it renders a service to the entire business community. In this conception doubt was due to the fact that the speculative market does offer an opportunity for the blind guesser who buys and sells on tips and hunches. He, of course, is gambling exactly as if he were betting on a horse race, and he doesn't last long unless he has unusually large resources. The majority of the men who are buying and selling speculative stocks to-day are operating on a more intelligent basis.

The stock market itself presents three distinct phases. In its movement it can be compared with an ocean.

The first movement consists of the day-to-day fluctuations which move prices of stocks up or down a fraction of a point and are similar to the ripples;

they come and go with the breezes, are logically manipulated and artificial, and cannot be foreseen in any way. The day-to-day trader who tries to get in and get out with a few dollars ahead is doomed to disappointment. The market is rigged against him. As soon as he and a number of his fellows have bought, the price is pushed down, and when they have been scared out it goes up again.

The second phase of the market comprises the intermediate movement of a few points in one direction or the other which extends over several days or several weeks. They are very similar to the waves of the ocean and cannot be forecasted any more accurately than can the day-to-day movement. In most cases they are manipulated, tips are circulated, the stock is pushed up artificially, the general public seeing it rise buys in at the top, then the insiders pull the string, the stock goes down, the public gets scared and sells out, and the insiders have cleaned up. Rather than try to play the day-to-day movement or the week-to-week and intermediate phases of the market, you had better try Monte Carlo. In spite of the fact that the " house " there is fixed so that you have a handicap of 2 per cent. you still have a much greater chance for your money than you have in the speculative market.

The broad movements of the market, however, are governed by the same fundamental laws which govern and cause business changes. Over a period of years the whole market rises and falls with consistency. What is more, these periods can be estimated with considerable accuracy. If you have but the patience to operate in accordance with fundamental conditions, you can buy in a depression zone, hold until the whole market has risen and distribution is in process, selling in an over-expansion zone. By keeping your funds liquid on the down-swing you avoid the loss sustained by those who are not operating in accordance with fundamental conditions. You have your cash ready to buy in again at the bottom.

This makes it not only a certain and greater profit than that of the average day-to-day trader, but in following it you are also of distinct service to the business world. To begin with, the period of accumulation, the first stage of the speculative long swing, invariably comes during a period of business depression. Surface conditions in business are naturally and invariably discouraging, industrial profits are small, and the prices of industrial stocks are very low. The average man is pessimistic and would not buy if he had anything left to buy with. The long-swing speculator comes into the market at this time with cash in hand and he buys his stocks at a ridiculously low figure. In lending his support at this critical time he also tends to stem the tide of the depression and to lend a certain amount of confidence to a badly disorganized and discouraged business world.

The average speculator who is inclined to worship the " here and now " theory has seen these same

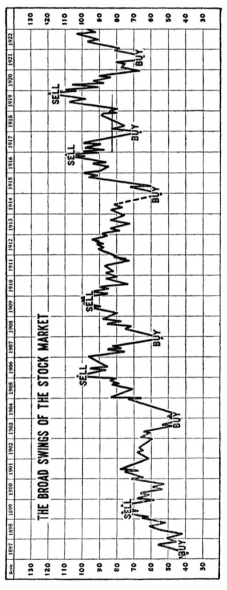

Broad Savings of Stock Market — 1897–1922

stocks come down from a high level. In fact, he has probably lost money on them all the way down. Business in general is wavering and hesitant, industrial profits are very small, if there are any at all. He cannot be convinced that *that* is the time to buy. The man who has courage and a knowledge of fundamental conditions, however, is not deterred by these surface conditions; he buys his stocks and trims his lamp for the feast that is to follow.

Following this period of accumulation comes the phase of rising prices. Even before business improvement is definitely indicated in actual industrial earnings, the stock market hears rumors of increased activity and increased profit. As stock prices rise, the long-swing speculator begins to pile up larger paper profits and the stocks keep on rising. There is a temptation to sell, but fundamental conditions indicate that the top has not been reached. In the meantime, the discouraged outsider begins to sit up and take notice, as he watches the stocks rise. Later in this period, after they have risen to a point where they are no longer in the strictly bargain class, this same average speculator can't stand it any longer, and he buys in possibly twenty-five points higher than the level at which the long-swing speculator purchased his holdings.

As the general public comes into the market and business conditions begin to improve we travel the trend up into the period of expansion. Another display of courage is here called for. The long-pull buyer has arrived at the time when he must sell his holdings, now showing good profits, and get his capital into liquid form. He must do this in spite of coming business, rapidly spreading prosperity, strong and active stock and commodity markets, and a rampant enthusiasm on every hand. These times are really distinctly unfavorable; they are the danger signal which tells the coming of another period of depression. They mean that prosperity having arrived has been overdone as usual, that a period of depression will follow, and that it will be overdone. The long-swing operator, therefore, sells his stocks at good prices and puts his money in the bank. He has made from 25 per cent. to over 100 per cent. on his money.

The average speculator in the meantime has made some money during the last half of the rise. With such evidence of prosperity, however, he cannot be convinced that it is time to sell. He believes that things are going to keep right on going up, hence he continues to add to his holdings, and when the break comes, indicating the beginning of a period of declining prices, he is completely wiped out or is forced to carry a list of high-priced stocks over a period of three to five years down through the period of decline until he gets into another period of prosperity, when he may be able to sell them for what they cost him. Ordinarily he will carry them all the way down and then sell them out at the bottom, unless he has absorbed some wisdom in the meantime.

Returning now to our long-pull operator we may say that with the cultivation and exercise of the two qualities — courage to buy and to sell, and patience to hold — and with the lesson learned that the market discounts the future, the present being a faulty basis for speculation, the mastery of a few simple rules is all that is necessary to turn out the successful speculator.

First and foremost, one should remember that in every major movement of the market there are numerous minor phases. These positively should be ignored. They are without significance, have their basis in surface and not fundamental conditions and the attempt to follow them consistently is likely to be as injurious to one's financial operations as the dope habit is to one's character. Trying to ride up and down with every rally and decline in the stock market will destroy every conviction based on sound fundamental principles one might have held at the beginning. These rallies and declines, as we have just said, have their basis in surface conditions, temporary developments of momentary importance only, contrasting with the long-pull or major movements that are controlled by the fundamentals. Surface conditions are usually a reflection of the " here and now " which we have referred to heretofore. They indicate the action of current developments such as the publication by some company of a good or a poor report, political doings, crop news, and other happenings of the day.

The technical position of the market itself has much to do with these temporary rallies and declines. By " technical position " I mean the volume of stocks held on the long or short side by the " public." If there has been a period of rising prices, during which much bullish propaganda has been circulated and pools or stock syndicates have disposed of their holdings, there may be a succession of bear attacks or short selling for the purpose of depressing prices and influencing the public mind to sell, which is not a very hard task. On the other hand, if the market has been declining for a few days or longer, conditions may be ripe for a rally, and with the aid of a little bullish propaganda the weak short interest is run in and prices recover half or perhaps all they have lost in the preceding period of decline. Anyone who can definitely tell what form such movements will assume and when they will break out would have child's play in explaining the theory of relativity and the fourth dimension to a kindergarten class. The best safeguard against the influence of the short swing is, having once adopted a position in accordance with the fundamentals, to forget the market entirely.

Another pitfall of which one must beware is the partial payment or margin method of trading. It would, of course, be wrong to assume that all margin traders lose money. It is undeniably true, however, that a liberal majority of the speculators who come to grief do so because they had been holding their stocks with some stranger's money. The weakness of the margin method is contained in this one fact — that by operating with borrowed capital a dependent position is necessarily assumed. Holding stocks with one's own capital, on the other hand, permits maintenance of a strictly independent position. Independence, furthermore, is an excellent tonic for one's peace of mind, a state which few margin traders ever enter.

To take up another phase of this subject, margin trading may be said to lead to over-trading. This practice is, in simple language, biting off more than one can chew. Consider the case of a man who puts up $10,000 as a margin to buy a list of stocks. The market begins to appreciate and soon shows him a paper profit of, say, $2,000. The next step is the employment of this $2,000 to buy more stocks, since it is so easy for this man to make money in stocks. It is not long, however, before the inevitable shake-out or short-swing reaction occurs, brought on by some passing development, turning the $2,000 surplus into a $2,000 deficit. Whereupon to satisfy his broker's call for margin it becomes necessary to sell the additional stocks he bought and as well some of the original commitments, all, very likely, at a loss, since margin calls never come when stocks are going up. This is not the invariable practice, for some have the courage to forego " pyramiding " or the use of paper profits as margin, but it is common enough to warrant the conservative operator in shunning altogether the method that so many others have tried and found wanting.

The practice of selling stocks short is still another example of *how not to do it*. This method seems just about as plausible and is more dangerous than margin trading. The theory is that, if one can make money by buying stocks and holding them during the course of a bull market, or period of rising prices, why isn't it just as possible to profit by reason of a decline in stock prices, or a bear market, through the medium of short sales, or selling what one does not own? Admittedly this theory sounds attractive, but, among others, it has one very glaring weakness. It fails to take account of one's inability to determine just when the bear market is to begin. A sale just a little too soon may mean the loss of a fortune. One may consistently ask why this is so. The answer is not hard to give.

The end of every bull market or distribution period is featured by wild manipulation. Prices of individual stocks are whirled up to dizzy heights. Not infrequently the stocks of least merit and poorest industrial position are shot up as high as the others in this manipulative orgy. Hence, the failure to anticipate correctly the end of the period by even so short a margin as a week or two may mean that one has a short position on stocks at levels 50 or 100 points lower. The average temperament cannot stand such a strain as this; so the common result is a rush to cover at or not far from the peak. In a short-sale transaction, moreover, one's potential losses are unlimited, while in a long transaction one can never lose more than the number of points one paid for the holdings. By and large, short selling is hazardous business and even the man with unlimited nerve and substantial purse frequently is caught. Others would do well to confine their speculation to outright commitments on the long side. So much for the pitfalls, — short-swing speculation, margin trading, and short selling.

Now, is it all that one needs, to have a knowledge of fundamental conditions and their relation to the stock market as well as to be aware of the weaknesses in the fabric of speculation? Not entirely so. We must emphasize the need of knowing *how* to buy stocks as well as *when*.

This seems too elementary, one will say. All that is needed is to make up one's mind to buy and then give one's order to the broker to be executed. True, but much depends upon how one apportions funds among the different stocks.

First, let us say that it is necessary to hold a considerable number of different stocks and different classes of stocks in speculating for a long pull. The reason for this is that while fundamental conditions exercise their influence on the movements of the market as a whole, none can say which particular stocks or class of stocks will participate most or least in the upward trend. For all stocks do not move alike by any means. The solution of the problem is found in the arrangement of purchases in such a way as to include as many as possible different issues and different groups of issues. By this method one is placed in the position of profiting by the average movement of the entire list.

It would, of course, be very gratifying if one could single out a special stock or special classes of stocks as more likely to share in the upward movement than others. This, however, cannot be accomplished any more readily than by accurate analysis of the short-swing movements of the market. Concentrating one's attention and capital on a single issue is speculation on the basis of guesswork. If one is willing to go into the market on such a basis, it would be better by far to place one's affairs in the hands of trustees and go into seclusion. The wise and conservative policy is to " spread out all over the board," making only one reservation. This one reservation is the selection of seasoned rather than unseasoned issues and groups.

Every expansion period witnesses the formation of a multitude of new companies and the launching of new industries. Some manage to stay on for a few years or longer and others quickly give up the ghost. It is best to shun them all until they can be placed in the class of well-seasoned companies or lines of business of known record of accomplishment. With this one reservation, however, as many different stocks and different groups that are in a sound position as one's capital will permit should be incorporated in one's list. To be sure, you may pick one or two bad ones, but the small amount involved will have little effect on the final result. Better a holding of twenty-five stocks with one disappointment than the singling out of two stocks with the risk that one-half of your entire investment be lost.

POSSIBILITIES OF PROFIT IN LISTED STOCKS

To those unfamiliar with the long swings of the stock-market, it may seem impossible to increase one's principal from about $6,000 to over $600,000, or to 100 times its original value. This is equivalent to the increase given by an interest rate of over 15 per cent. compounded semi-annually. Statistics show, however, that such profits are theoretically possible. In actual practice even the most experienced investors have not always been able to pick the lowest month of the market for buying or the highest month for selling. *They do not always come nearer than 10 per cent. to the low and high points. Even so they make very substantial profits. In fact, in some cases they do better than the following table suggests.* Moreover, as fundamental statistics become more complete and more soundly interpreted, investors can approach nearer and nearer to the profits outlined below. The following tabulation traces the long swings of the stock market averages. It shows in successive steps the potential rewards of service rendered by helping to steady business conditions.

That there might be no possibility of bias, the selection of stocks is confined to the Dow, Jones market averages of 20 industrials (12 industrials prior to the stock market closing in 1914) and of 20 rails, from 1896 to date. It has been necessary to carry back these averages to 1892, retaining in so far as possible, the same stocks that Dow, Jones used. Selection was not made of the lowest point of these averages for purchase, nor the highest point for sale, for in the exercise of ordinary judgment it is impossible to pick the absolute lows and highs. Instead there was assumed a purchase at the average price of the rail group and of the industrial group for the low month of the stock market movement, and a sale at the corresponding average prices of the high month of each swing. There was bought the same number of shares of each stock in the average, except where there was a balance of capital remaining which would enable the investor to purchase one additional share each of all the rails, or of all the industrials which make up the average.

In 1893 the purchase of four shares each of the rails and 5 shares each of the industrials required, with commissions, a total of $6,046. Dividends and rights while the stocks were held, and interest at savings bank rates on these dividends to April, 1899,

CONSTANT CONSISTENT PROFITS

1893 July	Original principal invested @ 49.09 for rails, @ 34.22 for industrials....		**6,046**
	Dividends and interest @ 4%		
1899 April	Stocks bought 7/'93, sold @ 85.80 for rails, @ 74.94 for industrials		
	Investment to date (including balance on interest)..............		13,359
	Interest 1 year @ 3¾% on investment to date		
1900 June	Available for stock purchase @ 76.49 for rails, @ 56.53 for industrials..		13,865
	Dividends, and interest @ 3½%		
1901 June	Stocks bought 6/'00, sold @ 116.02 for rails, @ 77.17 for industrials....		
	Investment to date (including balance on interest)..............		20,618
	Interest, 2 years @ 3½% on investment to date		
1903 Nov.	Available for stock purchase @ 91.95 for rails, @ 43.81 for industrials..		22,101
	Dividends, and interest @ 3½%		
1906 Jan.	Stocks bought 11/'03, sold @ 135.36 for rails, @ 98.72 for industrials ..		
	Investment to date (including balance on interest)..............		39,033
	Interest, 1½ years @ 3½% on investment to date		
1907 Nov.	Available for stock purchase @ 84.27 for rails, @ 55.74 for industrials..		41,094
	Dividends, and interest @ 3¾%		
1909 Aug.	Stocks bought 11/'07, sold @ 131.59 for rails, @ 97.78 for industrials		
	Investment to date (including balance on interest)..............		71,689
	Interest, 2 years @ 4% on investment to date		
1911 Sept.	Available for stock purchase @ 111.96 for rails, @ 76 61 for industrials.		77,598
	Dividends, and interest @ 4%		
1912 Oct.	Stocks bought 9/'11, sold @ 121 96 for rails, @ 92.24 for industrials		
	Investment to date (including balance on interest)..............		91,990
	Interest, 2 years at 4% on investment to date		
1914 Dec.	Available for stock purchase @ 89.85 for rails, @ 54.97 for industrials..		99,573
	Dividends, and interest at 4%		
1915 Dec.	Stocks bought 12/'14, sold @ 106.47 for rails, @ 97.00 for industrials		
	Investment to date (including balance on interest)..............		144,253
	Interest, 2 years @ 4% on investment to date		
1917 Dec.	Available for stock purchase @ 75.31 for rails, @ 70.17 for industrials..		156,144
	Dividends, and interest @ 4¼%		
1919 July	Stocks bought 12/'17, sold @ 88.26 for rails, @ 109.70 for industrials		
	Investment to date (including balance on interest)..............		233,528
	Interest, 1½ years 4¼% on investment to date		
1921 June	Available for stock purchase @ 68.95 for rails, @ 69.21 for industrials..		248,734
	Dividends, and interest at 4½%		
1923 Mar.	Stocks bought 6/'21, sold @ 88.89 for rails, @ 103.87 for industrials		
	Investment to date (including balance on interest)..............		377,918
	Interest, ½ year @ 4½% on investment to date		
1923 Oct.	Available for stock purchase @ 79.23 for rails, @ 88 11 for industrials..		386,421
	Dividends, and interest @ 4½%		
1925 Oct.	Stocks bought 10/'23, quoted @ 103.23 for rails, @ 150.65 for industrials		
	Investment to date...		**654,240**

totaled $2,065.   Upon selling in April 1899, the
same stocks (less commissions and taxes) brought
$11,294, giving a total principal at that date of $13,-
359.   Placing this sum on deposit for one year, the
current savings bank interest brought $506, giving a
total principal of $13,865 for investment at the next
low month of the market, in June, 1900.

CHAPTER XVI

BUSINESS PROBLEMS

IF you will look over the community in which you were born it will be found to have this general history: families rise and fall; industries change and the city or village must either go ahead or go backward. Nothing stands still in this world. Everything is a question of comparison. Unless there is progress there is deterioration; in fact, there must be a certain amount of progress to offset the inevitable depreciation. Therefore, one does not need to study fundamental conditions simply for the purpose of increasing his business. A knowledge of fundamentals is needed for purposes other than mere money making. A man must know fundamentals in order to exist and to hold his present position in the march of progress. Therefore, in these final chapters let me review briefly the various features already taken up in this book. Let us analyze in a general way the reason for failures, and from these reasons draw constructive plans for our own work.

Labor Conditions:

The study of declining businesses shows that a misunderstanding of the labor problem is an important factor in causing men to lose their businesses. This applies both to the old generation and to the new generation. The old generation was brought up on the "master and servant" principle. The old families drew a broad black line between employer and employee. So long as they had what they called "faithful workers"—workers without courage and ambition—they were happy and prosperous. They understood handling these docile employees who looked up to their employers intent only upon carrying out their orders. These were the kind of workers they had in the "good old days"—workers who seldom asked for more pay, who were satisfied with their condition, and who were content with the industrial system of their day.

Without doubt the old industrial system had many good features. In those days men and women were willing to do what they could do best, and manual labor was looked upon as honorable. People expected to work and enjoyed work. Producing and creating was a pleasure. They did not work long hours because they were forced to do so, but because they enjoyed the work and preferred it to staying at home, which was often the only alternative. In this way conditions have changed for the worse. It is very unfortunate that to-day work is looked upon by so many as something to be avoided. Furthermore, the prevalent custom of doing as little as possible in a day is a basic reason for high prices and generally unsettled conditions. In many ways employers are justified in wishing that the " good old days " and the good old labor conditions were back.

The employers of those days, however, did make a mistake in resisting instead of recognizing the changed conditions, especially as it was not a new thing to have changed conditions. There has been a constant change in the relation of employer and employee since the days of feudalism and slavery. A constant evolution has been going on during the past thousand years, and there has been just as much change during the past generations as during previous generations. This change will continue. Why should it stop suddenly with our generation? The employers who have recognized this change and have adapted themselves to it have continued in business. Most of those who have bucked the change have fallen by the wayside. That the readers of this book may recognize that these changes are inevitable is my earnest desire.

Let us not be just as disgusted with the next generation as the old generation was disgusted with us. As we attempted to start where our parents left off, so our children will attempt to start where we leave off. As we struggle to better our conditions, so our employees may likewise struggle to get away from us and be independent. Of course, in such action they take distinct risks, as a large proportion of those starting new businesses fail. But their purpose in so attempting is good, and we should not blame them for it.

During the past twenty years we have seen labor unions develop to an amazing extent. These are often repulsive to those who have built up a business without being hampered by labor leaders. But the labor union is as inevitable as the income tax. When labor unions are universal all will be affected alike, and no one concern will be worse off than are its competitors. The next generation will take labor unions for granted, but they will have new problems with which to contend. Socialism, I. W. W.'-ism, Bolshevism, or some other kind of "ism" will disconcert the young business men of twenty years hence. The important point for us to realize is that there will always be something for us to contend with along labor lines. The labor problem always has existed and always will be with us. Moreover, I would not give much for a people who were not striving to better themselves, even though they may be doing it along uneconomic lines.

This does not mean that you should become actively interested in the labor movement, or try experiments in profit-sharing, shop committee management, or in any other untested ideas. It is just as foolish to attempt to lead the procession as it is to drag behind. The industrial system of the next generation may be some one of these systems which we now discuss or it may be something entirely different. No one knows to-day what will be the solution of the industrial problem, or what industrial system will be the next one adopted. My desire simply is that you recognize that the same business movements which we have been considering apply to labor and the relation between employers and wage workers. This labor movement is continually in progress. The successful business man will adapt himself to these changes and attempt neither to lead them nor to resist them.

In other places in this book reference has been made to two different movements in progress at the same time. There are the long-swing or great tidal movements, the short-swing or the wave movements. These two sets of movements apply to labor problems as to all others. There is the long-swing, covering a period of twenty to thirty years, and there are the shorter periods synchronizing with the Babsonchart. I have no fears as to the ultimate outcome of the struggle between employers and wage workers. Gradually those who have money will learn to give up, and those who have no money will learn to wake up. Employers will learn the lesson the radicals are trying to teach, and the wage workers will learn the lessons the employers are trying to teach. Those who have money will learn that their safety and prosperity depend upon others also being well off. Those who have not will learn that righteousness, industry, and thrift are the basis of all prosperity, and that we can all have more only as we produce more. Before that time comes, however, there will probably be more trouble and distress.

We refuse to learn except by experience and there is no reason why our employees should be different and wiser. Therefore, the present uneconomic labor conditions may be carried further and further until they bring about a catastrophe. Labor may continue its methods of uneconomic production and avoiding work until it has forced the world into an industrial chaos. Then, however, labor will come to its senses, and of itself start out on a new tack to increase production and render service. Then will follow a great era of prosperity for all interests and groups. This will continue until another generation which has not known of the vicissitudes of its ancestors comes into being. They will start out on some new " ism," attempting some still more radical experiment, and again there will be trouble. The next thousand years will probably see more progress than the last thousand years, but there will be, as in the past, ups and downs as the business areas develop. The man, however, who knows fundamentals, and the principles underlying these business movements, knows the period that he is in and the period that is to come, and can thus save himself from the troubles resultant from these industrial upheavals. Yes, more than this, he can capitalize them and profit by them if he only will.

Buying Commodities:

Another feature which has broken many previously successful business men has been an attempt by them to monopolize certain trade in their village, city, or country. An analysis of business men shows that the most successful of them do not deliberately set out to make money. They enjoy their business as you enjoy a game; and they fight in it as our ancestors fought for fish and fowl. Consequently, when such men accumulate money enough and a business which should satisfy them, they are no more contented than when they started. They love the game so much that they keep on playing and playing. Not being satisfied with their success, they try to swamp competitors, take on new lines, and start in new fields. In many cases this brings disaster.

Many of the large business failures have been due to an attempt to create monopolies, or to control the prices of certain raw materials or products. This has almost always proved a mistake. *Never in the history of the world has a permanent monopoly been established.* Corners have lasted only a short time. Much more money has been lost by attempting to control markets than has ever been made by that process. As you go forth into business may your motto be " Live and let live." Don't try to do all the business in your community or in your line. Never attempt to crush competitors. There is enough business for all. Business makes business. Our prosperity ultimately depends upon the other fellow's being prosperous also. In order for us to sell goods the other fellow must be able to buy. Let us help him prosper.

Instead of trying to make money by cornering the market, our great opportunity will be in traveling with the market. Most of the successful merchants are those who have studied fundamental conditions and have known *when* to buy. These men have not attempted to stop the ebb and flow of the tide, but rather have planned their merchandising to take advantage of the ebb and flow. This means that they have bought intelligently; they have studied and been guided by fundamental conditions. Either consciously or unconsciously they have watched the business cycles and planned their merchandising campaigns in accordance therewith.

It is an old saying that anything well bought is half sold. Certainly the greatest losses in business have come from over-buying, or from loading up at the wrong time in a business development. In a previous chapter I have showed that a few failures are a dangerous sign and many failures are a favorable sign, as far as future business is concerned. One chief reason for this is that people become very optimistic during a period of over-expansion. Having been caught with a shortage of goods, they determine never again to be so caught, and buy very heavily believing that the period of over-expansion will continue indefinitely. Having seen prices rise over long periods, they believe they will continue to rise; so they buy freely irrespective of prices. When the period of decline starts and the depression follows, such persons are caught with a great stock of goods purchased at high prices.

Study fundamental conditions in connection with your buying. The four periods of a business cycle apply equally as well to the prices of the things which you must buy as to the conditions of business itself. If the commodities in which you deal are now too low, you can be absolutely sure that some day they will be too high. If they are now too high in price, you can be absolutely sure that some day they will be too low again. The long-range price trend over a long period may be upward or downward, but the shorter trend is continuing in operation just the same. It is the movements due to these shorter trends — rather than the twenty-year trends — which interest men in active business.

Hence, the great importance of studying fundamental conditions when buying raw materials, manufactured products, and commodities in general. Instead of having this trend work against you and cause you losses the thing to do is to capitalize it and profit by it. The course of prices is much like a stream of water; one can row with it, or one can row against it. The ordinary man starting in business is like a farmer building a water wheel on a mill river. His success depends upon the way he sets the wheel. The important thing is to set the wheel so that the running stream will make it turn. The important thing in business is to use and profit by these business trends instead of ignoring them.

As great losses are brought about by refusing to recognize fundamentals, so great profits are possible through the study of fundamentals. This is especially true in connection with the purchase of raw material, merchandise, and commodities in general.

National Distribution:

I recently visited a city which has been famous for its manufacture of one product. Nearly all the factories are engaged in the manufacture of this product, and almost the entire income of the people depends on its sale. Owing to changed conditions this sale has been greatly hampered in recent years. Out of some twenty large concerns only one is prosperous to-day. The prosperity of this one concern is due to its selling methods. Its owner alone of all the manufacturers of the city recognized that they could no longer depend upon jobbers for the sale of their products. He alone insisted that the product must be sold direct to the consumer by mail. Against the advice of the older firms in the city, this young man burnt his bridges by severing his connections with the jobbers, and started to form a direct personal connection with consumers all over the country.

The first effect of any such change is naturally depressing. He lost much trade in the early days. He got the ill will of the jobbers and they in turn passed this ill will on to the retailers. The banks withdrew their credit, and for two or three years the situation looked bad. This man, however, was a student of fundamental conditions. He had studied the industry and the sales possibilities as an engineer would study a contour map. Without prejudice one way or the other, he had come to the conclusion that fundamental conditions in the market had changed. He found that the goods were now being purchased by a different class of people than those who were formerly the buyers, and for a different reason. He believed that the retailers no longer had the same incentive to push these special goods that they formerly had; but would naturally push a competing line that would sell more easily. Hence, he stuck to his proposition to sell direct by mail. Suddenly the tide turned in his favor. Orders came in at a tremendous rate. Success justified his study and conclusions. To-day his plant is running full time while most of the other plants in that city are shut down. And to-day he has the one successful business in that community, and is the one man there who is making money.

Yet I should not be surprised if in the next cycle he is superseded by some other firm. He is now getting on in years. Although he was the first man in his city to adopt national advertising and direct selling by mail, yet he is using the same original methods with which he started twenty-five years ago. Although he was the first to take an advanced step, yet he has been satisfied with this one step forward and has not taken a second or a third. He fails to recognize that conditions are continually changing, and are changing as much to-day as they changed in the years gone by. Twenty-five years ago he recognized changing situations and adapted himself to them. To-day, however, he is failing to recognize that further changes are still in progress. He is now as stubborn as were the other manufacturers twenty-five years ago. He cannot see the light of the future any more than they could see it in their day and generation.

Recognize fundamentals in connection with the selling of goods. Remember that evolution is continually in progress in connection with the natures and desires of men and women. The cities and communities where your goods could best be sold a few years ago may have the least need of them to-day. Yet there are many fertile fields where your products to-day are very much wanted. Hunt up these fertile fields. Business is always good somewhere. The business areas are continually developing but they travel gradually across the country north and south or east and west. The sun rises and sets once in every twenty-four hours, but it rises at different times in different places. When we in New England are eating our breakfast, the people in California are having their soundest sleep. When we in the East are going to bed, the people in the West are busy at work. It is the same with business. Although business revolves like the earth on its axis and every section has its day and night, yet the sun of prosperity is always shining somewhere. The student of fundamental conditions will always know where that bright spot is and there he will be selling his wares.

The selling of goods is very much bound up with the tastes, customs, and fashions of the people. These likewise are changing constantly in accordance with definite economic laws. We criticize women as being the slaves of taste, custom, and fashion, but can they help it? If they cannot help it, it is due to the fact that taste, custom, and fashion are governed by fundamental laws. If this is so, it is entirely possible to forecast the changes. This is being done to-day by many manufacturers and merchants. The study of past history and the relation between cause and effect is teaching these men to forecast tastes, customs, and fashions of a year, or even five years hence.

When I was a boy there was a great demand for salt fish. I clearly remember how my father always had a whole salt fish hung by the tail in the back entry. About so often Mother would go out and cut a piece off, and we would have what is known as a salt fish dinner. Those were great dinners consisting of codfish, potatoes, beets, and a gravy made sometimes of cream and eggs and other times of pork. Then followed a period when people refused to buy whole fish, and insisted on buying it cut up and " boned "; that is, with the bones removed. People still bought cod dried and salted, but they wanted it packed neatly in a little box. The fishing firms who were the first to recognize the change in this demand made a great deal of money. But those who said " A whole codfish is good enough for me and I guess it is good enough for anybody," went to the wall. Note, however, that the change in people's taste would not stop with the desire for " boned " codfish.

Mackerel came into the market and was very popular. A great demand developed for salt mackerel. Instead of being dried like cod and haddock, the mackerel were pickled by packing them in buckets with salt and water. These buckets were shipped all over the country. The man in the West who had been brought up as a boy in the East could take one of these salt mackerel from the pickle and have a broiled fish that reminded him of his boyhood days. So the demand for salt mackerel increased. Those firms that went into the mackerel business made a lot of money while those who stuck to the cod and haddock trade did not. However, after people became more prosperous they were no longer satisfied with salt mackerel. They wanted fresh mackerel and fresh halibut. Thus the fresh fish industry came to be developed. Fresh sea fish is today sent in refrigerator cars or even by parcel post from the coasts to all parts of the country. You can get as fine fresh mackerel in Chicago, St. Louis, or Denver as in Gloucester, Mass., or Portland, Maine. Many firms that are now in the fresh fish business are making money, but those who refused to recognize the change in conditions are having very dull business.

We find still another change in fish fashions. Recently I visited the plant of the largest fish concern in America. Only one department was at work full capacity. Upon asking the reason that this one department was busy and not the others, the reply came, " Because this is the ' Ready-to-Fry ' department." I went over to the building to see what was being done and there I found them cooking fish and potatoes, mixing them together and canning them. Each can contained sufficient to make six fish balls. This is the stage at which the fish business is to-day. While my father was satisfied with a whole cod tied by the tail, hanging on the back porch, my young people will buy fish only when it is cooked and mixed with potatoes, ready for immediate use.

We well might stop and talk on the laziness of the growing generation and insist that as codfish and salt mackerel were good enough for us they should be good enough for the generations to come. But we shall never make business successes by arguing along these lines. If we are to make a success in business, we should recognize these changing conditions and capitalize them instead of ignoring them. If you are not successful in your selling to-day, it is probably due to the fact that you do not recognize the business areas in your sales, and that you do not take advantage of the changes in territories, industries, tastes, customs and fashions.

Retail Merchandising:

What has been said thus far applies mainly to national distributors who are interested in selling the country as a whole. When it comes to the retailer in a given city the problem is more intricate and the need of studying fundamentals is even greater. I say this because the national distributor has such a wide territory that the law of averages works largely in his favor. This is not so true with the retailer, who is dependent upon a given community and a limited area for his market. A retailer, especially in a city with diversified interests, should study industries in connection with his merchandising. Moreover, a retailer — in a city like Brockton dependent upon shoes, or Havana dependent upon sugar, Memphis dependent upon cotton, or some of our western cities dependent upon agriculture, lumber, or mining — who is dependent for his trade on the prosperity of some one industry should give much attention to the study of industries.

Some industry is always prosperous. Even when business is poorest a merchant in New York, Chicago, or Philadelphia, or any large city can do good business by studying the industries of his city. In all large cities some one industry is always prosperous, and often several industries are prosperous. There are over 300 common lines of activity in this country, most of which are to be found in every city. There never is a time but that 10 per cent. of them are doing well and 5 per cent. of them are relatively prosperous. And 5 per cent. of 300 is fifteen. The able retailer will always seek out these fifteen or more industries and will purchase the goods that the people engaged in them will want and will buy.

Many merchants fail because they buy only goods which they themselves like, or which they think other people should buy. These are narrow-minded small merchants. The greatest merchants absolutely ignore their own tastes, wishes and prejudices. They do not attempt to *determine,* but rather to *interpret* the needs and desires of their customers. Nothing will help so much in this work of interpreting future demands as a study of industries, always watching for the industry which is over-expanding and the industry which is about to be prosperous.

All industries go through their own phases, but the phases do not necessarily coincide. I have in mind four industries each one of which is traveling through a movement. Each one of these industries in the course of eight years enjoys over-expansion, decline, depression, and improvement. But as I look over these industries to-day I find that each one of them is now in a different period. One industry is very prosperous, another is in a depression, the third is in. a period of decline, and the fourth is in a period of improvement. A student of fundamentals recognizes these changes and these facts. One who is interested in business trends

is keen enough to know that every industry has a
phase of its own. Hence, he studies industries, especially the industries of his own customers. He
is not content to know simply the elementary principles of merchandising. He delves into the great
fundamental forces controlling the business of his
city. He is able to forecast when each will be prosperous and when each will be depressed. He purchases goods to suit that industry which will next
be prosperous, and he advertises to solicit the trade
of those who are employed in that industry. In
this way he wastes no ammunition. He always has
on hand the goods which are wanted, and his trade
is constantly increasing.

Men are naturally ambitious. You, the readers
of this book, are ambitious, for otherwise you would
not bother to buy and study it. As men become
successful, however, there is a tendency for them to
rest on their oars. Having once carefully studied
their business they are prone to think that they
know all about it, forgetting that changes are constantly in progress. They are content to know their
own industry, but do not take the pains to study
other industries upon which their customers are absolutely dependent for the money with which to buy.
Hence, a merchant becomes rusty as he gets older
and his position in his community is gradually filled
by younger men who understand the needs of the
new generation.

It is especially important that we older men keep

up with the younger. We should associate with them and learn their wants and desires. It is especially important that we keep in touch with the new industries which have come into being since we were young. When I was a boy there was no automobile industry, no moving picture industry, and almost no electrical industry, although most readers of this book will take these industries for granted, assuming that they always existed. Remember that they are new and that other industries are developing all the time. Keep acquainted with the progress and growth of all new activities. Don't brand them merely as fads, but recognize them and capitalize them.

Business Budgets:

Finally every business man must realize that a good accounting department alone does not offer absolute assurance of financial success, unless it happens to be assigned to the work of developing a budget for the business. No matter to what department you assign the making of the budget, expenditure on the work is a sound investment.

In 1926 the Federal Administration ruled that the Director of the Bureau of the Budget would rank immediately next to Cabinet Officers and ahead of all Bureaus and Sub-Department Chiefs. This was very significant and striking. It emphasized the importance which the budgeting of Government expenses has come to assume. Budgeting was chosen as a way to lower Federal Taxes. The question at once arose:

If the Government can effect large savings by budgeting its expenses, why doesn't the average business man regard the problem of budgeting as equally important for his own business? It is daily becoming more obvious that concerns of all sizes and in all lines of industry will find that a business budget is remarkably helpful both in cutting costs and increasing income, thus leading to greater profits.

As the years go by, competition is becoming more and more intense, business men are being compelled by economic pressure to resort to the well-planned budget to turn an otherwise red-ink loss into a black-ink profit. It is a mistake to think that business budgeting is something that applies only to the great corporations. These big organizations of course were among the first to find out that budgeting is indispensable. Actually, however, the company which needs budgeting most is one of moderate capital and facilities because such a concern depends more upon skillful management than unlimited resources. In fact, the " little fellow " is the very one who can least afford NOT to budget his business.

In making a business budget the first step is to get a fairly correct idea of how much money is coming in. This can be estimated by examining gross income during the past few years and studying its normal growth in comparison with general business conditions. As actual income may vary either above or below the estimate, some of the expenses may be budgeted as a percentage of the gross rather than forecast as a fixed amount. Next, the expenses of the past few years should be analyzed and arranged under suitable headings. They then should be expressed as percentages of the gross earnings. It is especially important to analyze and budget inventories for the stock of goods and supplies carried. Such inventories should bear a definite proportion to the gross business. Advertising is an item which should receive a definite proportion of the gross and this percentage should be kept inviolate. In many instances when other expenses exceed the allotted amount, there is an unfortunate tendency to raid the advertising account.

With changing economic conditions the success of most businesses is becoming more and more dependent upon intelligent advertising, which is a powerful tool for breaking down sales resistance. The advertising account should be treated with especial care when compiling a business budget. Having divided the business expenses into groups and proportioned them to the gross income, in the light of past experiences it is comparatively easy to lay out a budget for the coming year. There is such variation of groups and details in different businesses that it is hardly practical to attempt in this book to set up specimen budgets. If possible every business man should find out what is the best practice in his general line of business. One thing, however, can be recommended for nearly every business, namely: there should be a " contingent fund." In spite of the most careful forecasts, unexpected expenses almost invariably arise and must be met. When there is any economy or saving under a budget head it can be added to this " contingent fund."

A business budget differs radically from the familiar budget of family living expenses or a budget of Government expenses. The business budget aims not merely to control expenses but to build up income. In fact, the budgeting of sales is of the utmost importance because experience shows that sales can often be greatly increased when the sales department is trying to reach or exceed a definite goal. Moreover, in laying out a sales budget according to the buying power of the various sales territories, localities are often uncovered which have never been developed to their real possibilities. Sales budgeting sometimes shows that salesmen have dissipated much of their effort and have only half cultivated certain fields that should handsomely reward a more intelligent campaign. Even the simplest of sales budgets should lead to a considerable increase in business over the results that have been obtained by ill-directed struggles.

In estimating the amount of sales to be expected for the coming period, — such as the next six months, before any sales estimate is finally accepted for the budget, serious thought should be given to points such as the following:

1. The trend of fundamental conditions and the outlook for general business.

2. The sales records of the product in question.

3. The extent to which a given rise or fall in general business tends to affect the sales of that particular product.

4. Whether the high points and low points of sales tend to come early, midway or late in the periods of general business expansion and readjustment.

5. The outlook for the various industries to which the product is sold.

6. The outlook for the different territories in which the product is distributed.

7. Prospective policies as to additions, eliminations and other merchandising changes.

8. Other influences such as style trends, competition, etc.

The question of whether to reduce or enlarge the working forces has always been a serious problem. If skilled workers are released just before a period of good business, production may be handicapped, because it is difficult to build up an adequate working force on short notice. It is not only hard to find competent employees, but even after they have been hired there is still the problem of training them and fitting them into the organization. On the other hand, a concern naturally hesitates to carry a big payroll through months of waiting for business to materialize. Of course, even the best budget has no magical power to foretell the future, but it does stimulate careful planning. It sets up sharply the question of whether the coming production requirements are likely to increase, hold constant, or decline.

In the case of some concerns budgeting has had a remarkable effect on labor policies. Haphazard hiring and firing has been replaced by a steady balancing of personnel with production. Not only has the violence of the business swings been reduced but even the seasonal changes in payroll have been lessened, — greatly to the advantage both of the company and the workers. Every concern, therefore, should budget its payroll both in total and according to departments. This is important at all times, whether general business is in a period of expansion or a period of readjustment.

Statistics show that few concerns continue to make satisfactory profits. "Satisfactory" means in comparison with the percentage of profits which capital can earn merely by investment in securities without the work and worry of running a business. Profit is the difference between income and expenses. By simple and practical business budgeting, income can be built up and expenses can be kept down. Plan your work, work your plan and profits will result.

Those who attempt to cut costs without the guidance of a budget are always in danger of doing more harm than good. Business history would doubtless show many examples of individual companies and perhaps entire industries which have been damaged by careless cutting of costs. The job of keeping down expenses should be analyzed and planned with the same intelligence and energy that are devoted to building up sales. Reckless economy is sometimes as fatal as reckless expenditures. When guided by a business budget you can " prune for greater growth." The fundamental purpose of a business budget should be positive rather than negative. It should enlarge income as well as reduce costs. Budget control can save many concerns from actual bankruptcy, strengthen weak companies, and enable strong companies to reach still higher levels of success.

Chapter XVII

INVESTMENT PROBLEMS

FEW people fully realize the losses which are encountered by business men in connection with their investments. Many who were successful in business and retired wealthy have since lost a large portion of their fortunes through carelessness and ignorance in connection with the investment of their money. This applies not only to those who have retired or inherited money, but also to the active business man of to-day. Most business men will spend months in making a few thousand dollars which they will "invest" in a few minutes. It is said that the average business man gives less time to the selection of an investment from a bond circular than he gives to the selection of a lunch from a menu card.

Business men should give even more time and study to the investment of money than to the making of it, as *money is harder to conserve than to accumulate.* And the business man and those who have inherited money should give great thought to fundamentals. It is absolutely essential, in connection with the safe and profitable investment of funds, to understand the business swing and to know what period we are in at any given time. You say, " John Jones has made a lot of money through investments and he knows nothing about fundamentals." That may be true, but the reason that John Jones has made a lot of money in connection with his investments is because he happened to invest at the right time. Moreover, the chances are that unless John Jones soon becomes a student of fundamentals he will some day invest at the wrong time, and he will lose a good part of what he has already made.

The fact that rich families of fifty years ago are today often extinct as to wealth and position does not mean that they failed in business. Many of these made successes in business and retired leaving fortunes to their families. Through unwise investments or failure to change their investments at the right time these fortunes have been lost, and the families are now stranded. In many instances the parents or grandparents invested in what was the best for their day. They bought New Haven Railroad at 200 a share, and Boston & Maine at a corresponding figure. These were looked upon as the most conservative investments of that time, and for many years they were justly so classified. Later the estates with these interests were perhaps bankrupt. New Haven, Boston & Maine, and many of the other high-class investments of that day went by the board, ceased paying dividends, and in most cases have been reorganized.

The fault was not in *buying* these investments

but in holding them indefinitely. The law of action and reaction applies to investments as it applies to families, commodities, and industries. The best investments of our father's day are mostly poor investments today. The best investments of today will probably be poor investments for our children to bank upon. The business swing is continually in progress. Those who recognize fundamentals and study fundamentals can prosper in connection with their investments, while those who ignore fundamentals are sure to lose.

No investments stand still. *Every investment is continually growing better or growing worse.* They have their length of life the same as individuals. One might say, they are born, they grow up, they mature, and they die. During their early years their mortality is very great, but those which exist a certain length of time mature, only to die ultimately. A student of investments does not buy securities of an industry until that industry is sufficiently established so that it will surely grow up; but later when it is matured, *he sells.* Many families have held on too long and lost all.

The most popular investments to-day probably will all pass over yonder. Yes — there is even reason to believe that some day the best of to-day will go the way of the best of a generation ago. Telephones will always be used, as are the railways and the trolleys, but as an investment the cream will some day be gone. Certain public utilities form a most popular field of investment to-day. At the moment I would rather buy some of these utility stocks than almost any other kind, but some day these industries will be overdone — or the public may step in and seize it — and the value of these securities will depreciate. A student of fundamentals changes his investments according to the changes of the business trend. He not only knows *when* to buy but he also knows *what* to buy. Only by having such knowledge can he avoid the pitfalls and profit by the changes in business conditions.

Don't take flyers. Avoid gambling. Shun tips of all kinds. Remember that the only way to make money in the stock market is by rendering service, and the only way to render service is to store up money when it is plentiful and then use it when it is scarce. This means that in a period of prosperity it is better to buy nothing at all but let your money accumulate until it is needed. Follow the process of the ice man, who cuts and stores ice in the winter when it is a nuisance, knowing that before the year is over people will be crying for it. Hence, I say, when business is good, speculation rampant, and everybody is making money in the stock market, keep out of the market. Be content to let your money accumulate, because the day will come again when that money will be in great demand.

Prosperity usually develops into a period of over-expansion, which is followed by a decline and depression. When this time arrives prices tumble, brokers fail, and panic rules on the stock exchanges. If you are a student of fundamental conditions you will know when this period has arrived, and that it is the time to buy. Then take the money which you have been accumulating and keeping in liquid form during prosperous times and use it for the purchase of securities. By so doing you can step into the breach when you are most needed, and enable your money to perform a real service. When you begin to buy you help stop the panic and help to keep others from failing. For performing this service you will receive a handsome profit. You will receive good interest on your investment and be able to sell at perhaps double the original cost.

Following every panic comes a period of depression when money again becomes plentiful, and securities again rise in value. Soon an improvement comes when stocks soar in price and everybody is talking prosperity. During this period the securities which you bought become very valuable. Every day prices are rising and your profits are increasing. Strangely, as prices rise, more people become interested in the stock market and it is easier to get people to buy. Only students of fundamental conditions have the courage to buy during panics, but during prosperous times the reverse is true. Almost every one wants to buy during a period of expansion, and the higher the prices the more anxious they are to get aboard. This is the time when the student of fundamentals sells. Sell everything at such a time. Get your money into liquid form and get ready for the next depression.

The average investor is like the farmer who might insist on planting his crops in the fall just because there happen to be a few warm days in October. The average investor is like one trying to sell straw hats at the North Pole, or warming pans at the Equator. The average investor is the shortest-sighted and the most foolish man the world has produced. Men succeed in business but fail when it comes to the investment of their profits. Men work hard for wages and then lose them all on some oil or mining scheme. Families save and sacrifice only to see their savings lost through some " attractive " investment.

I am interested in helping you, my readers, in adapting yourselves to all forms of changing business conditions. I want you to recognize the business trend in connection with your labor problems, buying problems, selling problems, and the study of industries in particular. But I am not so worried about your success in business as I am about your success in investing the money which you accumulate. Again, I say, *it is easier to make money than it is to keep it.* The dangers which beset you outside your business are far greater than the dangers which face you within your business, especially during your years of struggle. Hence, I am anxious that you study fundamentals in connection with the purchase and sale of securities, and in connection with all forms of investment.

Briefly this means five things:

(1) When purchasing, select a broad list. Don't put all your eggs into one basket. And neither should you use baskets that you know have holes in them just for the sake of having more than one. Select only securities which you know to be good, but don't depend upon any one. Always keep your funds invested in at least twenty different companies, and eight or ten different industries.

(2) Buy stocks during panics. This will mean that you are buying when other people are not buying. You will buy during the dark days when your friends think that business is going to the bow-wows. Remember that when you buy something for nothing, it is usually worth what it costs. When you do what everybody else is doing, you generally lose money. Hence, buy stocks during times of panic or depression. The rest of the time be content to study fundamental conditions, statistics, and charts, preparing for the opportunities which will some day be yours.

(3) Pay *outright* for everything you buy. Don't buy on margin. Keep away from studying the tape. You may have to borrow money for your regular business, but don't borrow any money for the purchase of securities. Only the man who is free from debt knows what it really means to be healthy and happy. You may have to get into debt at some time in the purchase of goods, but unless you are a dealer in securities never get into debt for the purchase or

sale of securities. That means buy outright and *never sell short.*

(4) When the period of prosperity comes, liquidate your holdings. Get your money into cash and keep your cash in liquid form. Many know when to buy but fail to know when to sell. It sometimes takes more courage to sell during a period of prosperity than to buy during a period of depression. A student of fundamental conditions knows when to do both. The man who watches the business trend will know when to buy and when to sell. When it comes to the purchase of bonds, four additional rules are worthy of study.

(5) When making permanent investments for security and yield, bonds are most desirable. Different groups of bonds, however, may be purchased for different purposes. The following classifications may be observed:

Business Men's Bonds; These are the bonds which yield the most and consequently have the least security. Business men, however, who will confine their purchases to junior liens of reorganized companies will secure a maximum of yield without much risk. Statistics show that 80 per cent. of the corporations offering securities have reorganized *once,* but that only 20 per cent. have reorganized *twice.* Therefore, one greatly reduces his liability of loss by purchasing bonds of a company which has been reorganized, especially when buying high yields.

Investment Bonds: These securities should either

be well-secured mortgage bonds recommended by high-grade bond houses, or else should be underlying liens of reorganized properties. Expansion in the railroad and public utility fields has brought many companies to a point where a strict first mortgage makes up a very small proportion of total indebtedness and where such bonds are selling to give very low yields. Often bonds designated as " First & Refunding " will be a first mortgage on the most up-to-date and best part of the property and a general mortgage on the rest. Many times these are wholly conservative. One should try to get as close to first mortgage security as possible but recognize that the name of a bond, *per se,* is not necessarily an indication of its quality. Earnings record and general outlook must receive due consideration. As stated above, one greatly reduces his liability to loss by purchasing securities of reorganized companies; but this liability is still further reduced by buying securities which have been through the reorganization undisturbed. Many such issues are listed on the New York Stock Exchange. Unless one buys investment bonds from a high-grade established bond house, it is wise to confine one's holdings to listed underlying liens of properties which have been once reorganized. This advice especially should be heeded by women and those who must carefully conserve their principal.

Bonds for churches, Libraries, Hospitals, and other Philanthropic Institutions: When buying for others one is subject to criticism. Therefore, it is advisable to purchase for others only securities which stand well in the popular mind. Although bonds of reorganized companies are usually intrinsically better, still they are not so recognized by people in general. Therefore, when investing the funds of some quasi-public institution it is well to confine one's purchasing to the bonds of what are considered the highest-grade corporations. Bonds of the Pennsylvania Railroad Company, the New York Central Railroad Company, or the Commonwealth Edison Company or Pacific Gas and Electric Company are illustrations of such investments. It is true that these properties may some day suffer the fate which befell the Boston & Maine Railroad Company and the New York, New Haven & Hartford Railroad Company. Nevertheless, when purchasing for others it is well to be governed by the general opinion rather than stake the funds of other people solely on one's own personal opinion.

Bonds for Trust Funds: When purchasing as a guardian or trustee under appointment by the court, one should be even more careful. None of the three classes of bonds above mentioned is entirely satisfactory for the investments of such trust funds. In certain states, such as Massachusetts, Connecticut, and New York, definite securities have been legalized. Court rulings in other states show the character of bonds available for such purposes. Bonds which are legal for the savings banks of the states are usually legal investments for trustees. As an illustration of such bonds may be mentioned United States Government Liberty bonds, state bonds, and municipal bonds of the more conservative cities. Certain railroad and public utility bonds are also legal in some states for such purposes.

Business is guided by fundamental laws the same as are the movements of the planets and the changing of the seasons. A man may make a meagre living through industry and thrift without regard for these great fundamental laws of business. Millions of men are born, live, and die, without ever hearing of business phases. If, however, you are to become more than a drudge, if you are to have the joy of being a factor in production and distribution, you must not be content with merely working and saving. You must study and capitalize fundamentals.

I know of a family that for years lived on the Hudson River by some rapids. Generation after generation looked out on those rapids but they did no more than look. They drudged and saved, trying to make wheat and potatoes grow on the hillside bordering the river. Finally a young man of the fourth generation came back from an eastern college imbued with a desire to use those rapids for the development of power. His family laughed at him. They said that the rapids had always been there and always would be there, and any dam that he could erect would be washed away. He learned through mechanics that the same laws govern both the stream and the stability of dams. He believed that he could depend upon those laws, not only to get the power, but also to build a dam that the river would not wash away. At last he convinced others of his project, and it was finally developed. He was not only made wealthy but he was able to supply light and power to the whole vicinity, making the homes more cheerful and the work of the housewives easier.

The same opportunities exist for you today. There may be no undeveloped water powers, unfelled forests, or undiscovered mines in your vicinity, but the law of gravitation applies everywhere, and the law of the business trends applies everywhere. The time will come, generations distant, when this Law of Action-Reaction will be so universally used that the present fluctuations will be largely eliminated. When every one knows about business trends and applies that knowledge there will be but little opportunity for you to capitalize it and render service by its use. But until that time comes a great opportunity for service and profit exists in the study of fundamental conditions and business trends.

Chapter XVIII

A CONTINUOUS WORKING PLAN FOR YOUR MONEY

WHEN you study the actual security lists of thousands of investors, you find a most interesting and significant fact. You can divide investors into two well-defined groups. In the first group are those whose holdings are gradually losing value, their lists at present are worth less than 10 years ago; and 10 years from now they will probably be worth less than to-day. In the second group are those whose holdings are constantly growing in value. Year after year the lists of such investors continue to *appreciate* instead of *depreciate*. What causes this remarkable difference? Why are some investors always getting poorer while others are constantly getting richer?

Almost invariably the difference is right here: the investors who are losing ground are those who operate aimlessly; the investors who are steadily bettering their conditions are those who have a definite and continuous working plan for their money. In other words, by testing thousands of causes, it has been demonstrated that the foundation of investment success is a definite program. People don't try to construct a building without first getting a blue-print, even a small project like a chicken house can be carried out more successfully if you first make at least a rough sketch. The design of machinery, industrial enterprises of all kinds, agriculture, warfare, — in fact practically every human undertaking of any importance — is based upon a plan. Why is it, then, that so many investors expect to get along in a hit-or-miss way utterly devoid of systematic methods?

The following policy is necessarily general. Each person must fit these fundamental principles to meet his own particular conditions, requirements, and temperament. Moreover, this particular outline is not presented as necessarily ideal but rather to show in a specific and practical way some of the things which the typical investor should aim to accomplish in his program.

The first step in a continuous working plan for your money is to consider what funds you will have available for securities, after you have taken care of the needs of your business or profession, your household budget, your insurance, real estate and other requirements. When you have thus estimated the funds you will have available for securities, you are then ready to study three suggested methods of investigation. These may be summarized as follows:

(I) Buying and selling a broad list of stocks in accordance with fundamental conditions. That is, you buy such stocks outright in a period of depression, you sell in a period of prosperity, and then you hold your funds in liquid form until the next period of depression.

(II) This method is to invest in bonds for safety of principal with regular and assured income. Profit from rise in price is at most incidental.

(III) This method consists of carefully selecting stocks in fundamentally sound growing companies to hold for a long term. Intermediate price movements are not especially regarded and reliance is placed chiefly on the expected growth of the company over a stretch of years.

Of these Three Methods, Method I (buying and selling in accordance with periods of fundamental expansion and depression) has been discussed in Chapter XV. Method II (buying bonds primarily for safety of principal and income) has been treated in Chapter XVII. In regard to Method III (buying stocks of companies for the future) the following points are worth noting. Method III has distinct advantages and when joined with Methods I and II rounds out a continuous working plan for your money. This method consists of selecting stocks in companies, which over a term of years should enjoy a substantial and well-sustained growth. Even though you may be investing the bulk of your funds according to Methods I and II it is a good idea to have some stocks, which you intend to hold without especial reference to the periodic swings of fundamental conditions.

Such stocks, when judiciously selected, eventually

develop into very profitable holdings, partly because of the basic expansion in the industries, which
they represent. Some of the most prominent per-
sonalities in the industrial world almost never trade
in the stocks of their companies; nevertheless, such
holders have profited immensely from the growth
of their respective companies.

In Method I you are guided primarily by the position and trend of fundamental business conditions.
Under that method your chief concern is to buy a
broad list of good stocks at a time when general business is depressed and to sell these stocks when business again rises and a period of over-expansion develops. In Method III, however, you often have an
opportunity to buy stocks more in accordance with the
so-called net growth of business than with the periodic fluctuation above and below this line of net
growth. Such stocks as already remarked should be
selected in industries which are constantly expanding.
An advantage of this method appears in years such
as 1926, for example. In that year business had
expanded to a level where the conservative policy
was to hold most of your funds liquid. The average
of all stocks had previously reached a high zone.
Nevertheless, there are certain industries which continue to expand; and for this reason it was advantageous to hold a few stocks that were chosen from
the long growth viewpoint. Of course, whenever
there comes a broad downward movement in the
stock market even these " long growth " issues tend

to decline in company with all the others. You must clearly foresee temporary declines and must make up your mind that they will not sway you from your confidence in the underlying status of the securities that you have chosen. Of course, the opportunities to purchase stocks for a long growth are much more attractive during a period of depression than when prices have been inflated by a period of prosperity.

Under Method I you render a real economic service by helping to iron out the reckless booms and the equally disastrous slumps. In a similar way by holding certain stocks under Method III you help to stabilize the securities of younger industries which fundamentally are bound to grow over a period of years. Both of these Methods, therefore, are justified economically since they enable you to render a definite service and promote true prosperity. As a rule, you should use this long growth Method III in conjunction with the other two methods previously described. Moreover, in most cases this long-growth method should be applied to a relatively smaller proportion of one's funds than is devoted to either Method I or Method II. In combination with the other two methods, the long-growth method enables you to avoid intervals of apparent inactivity and enables you to take advantage of especial opportunities at all times; and the profits to be gained are well worth while.

It has already been pointed out that the first step in determining how much money you can devote to the purchase of securities is to decide how much you require for other purposes. The professional man, for example, must provide for office rent, salaries of assistants, equipment, and various other expenses. When considering professional work, it is significant that professional men as a group are gradually becoming more interested in the study of fundamental economic trends of various localities, to ascertain in which cities or towns there will be the greatest opportunities for service for engineers, architects, physicians, dentists and other professional men.

They are finding that the professional man's collections often bear a very close relationship to the trend of local business, rising when the locality swings upward into prosperity and declining when the locality sinks downward into depression. Professional men also tend now to make a closer study of accounting methods, efficiency and other matters of applied economics. They are finding that a thorough knowledge of practical economics strengthens rather than impairs professional attainments.

Many investors when allocating funds for the purchase of securities must do so with reference to business requirements. Prospective needs for large sums in a man's business will mean a lessened amount available for securities. In connection with business operations it is convenient to consider these under the following three heads: (1) Buying; (2) Selling; (3) Management. Buying and selling are the primary operations of business and they are united by the connecting link of management. In fact, with modern methods of accounting, the budget of a business may often be laid out almost in accord with these lines. The funds which will be required for buying goods or buying raw materials to be made into goods; funds which will be required for operating the sales department; and finally funds which will be needed for overhead and administrative costs of management: all these must be estimated.

The amount of funds available for securities will also depend upon how much money the investor will require for his household and personal budget. In this budget there appear, of course, the elementary items of food, shelter, and clothing. There appear also the item of operating and maintenance and a general classification to cover miscellaneous expenses, such as education, travel, charities, etc. In a broad way these items do not tend to increase in proportion to the growth of income. In the case of very large incomes such budget items as we have mentioned may be fairly small percentages. As the income increases the items which show the greatest relative expansion are usually the savings and insurance.

Nearly every investor, however, whether large or small, is interested in insurance and his requirements for this purpose help to determine the amount which he will have available for the purpose of buying securities. Insurance might be regarded by some authorities from the standpoint of either investment or protection. The subject of insurance as an investment will take us too far afield and at present we are referring to insurance primarily as protection. That is its real function.

There is another requirement which must be considered when the average investor is reckoning the funds which he will devote to securities. Numberless investors are interested in real estate. Real estate may be purchased primarily for income or primarily for profit. This is a large subject in itself and can hardly be touched upon adequately at this point. It is important to note, however, that the trend both of rentals and real estate prices has a very close relationship to the trend of local activity as a whole.

The real estate buyer therefore should make a close and constant study of economic development of his locality from two viewpoints: first, the locality's long-pull growth over a stretch of many years; second the shorter swings as local business rises from a period of depression. In other words, like the buyer of securities the buyer of real estate must watch fundamental conditions closely with particular emphasis, of course, upon local as well as national trends.

Besides the management of his own funds, nearly every investor has certain responsibilities for the funds of others. The average investor, for example, holds a position of responsibility as a director of banks or industrial corporations, as a trustee of institutions, the executive of estates, a guardian, member of investment committees, building committees, and numberless other activities of this kind. Many men feel that when thus entrusted with responsibility for the funds of others, it is more than ever desirable to provide themselves with the most conservative and comprehensive service obtainable.

As never before, far-sighted investors are keeping a close watch upon the trend of scientific discoveries and inventions. There is a two-fold necessity for this vigilance. In the first place existing investment values may be very rapidly upset by some forward step in scientific and technical progress. For example, the older branches of the textile industry were radically affected by the introduction of rayon. There were important reactions in the paint industry following the introduction of the new enamels. Radio had a profound effect upon the phonograph industry. In the second place every important invention and discovery not only brings about changes in existing securities, but makes valuable, far-reaching opportunities in new industries. The investor, therefore, should keep himself thoroughly informed in such matters. Failure to do so means that he will not only miss great opportunities but will expose himself to equally great dangers.

The question may be asked whether scientific and technical inventions and discoveries have not always been of importance to the investors. It is true, of course, that the progress of science has been going on for many years and has long been a factor in the investment situation and outlook. Science, however, is now moving ahead at an accelerated pace. Each new discovery and invention has a multitude of reactions and each of these in turn leads to still further forward steps. There is a snowball growth or multiplication in geometric ratio, so that in the future, even more than at present, it will be necessary for the investor to keep himself informed on the longer and longer strides which science is making.

Moreover, some of the very discoveries which at first seem to be of merely theoretical interest may prove to have the most practical bearing and the most immediate effect upon investment dangers and investment opportunities. Therefore, it cannot be emphasized too strongly that the investor should vigilantly scrutinize the work of chemists, physicists, and other scientists and technicians. Your present holdings which now seem so impregnable may rapidly shrink in values while new opportunities will presently appear in fields which are now remote or unknown.

Chapter XIX

CONCLUSION

THIS final chapter is being written in the city where I was born and brought up. Yes, in the very pasture where I drove the cows when a boy! The first twenty-two years of my life were spent here, and I come back to it every summer. Its people are a fine sturdy race, accustomed to struggles, yet hospitable and optimistic. It was a fine place in which to bring up a lad. Every boy was trained to work and save, as there were very few natural resources. Nature provided only rocks, bushes, and the opportunity to catch fish from the ocean which pounds the shore. Most cities are surrounded by fertile fields, verdant forests or rich mines; but my home was favored with none of these natural resources. Every dollar that its people earned came from hard labor either on rocky hillside farms, or on the ocean where many men went never to come back. These difficulties, however, made men strong and independent.

Yet wealth was made even under these trying circumstances. There were many rich families on the Cape during my boyhood days; in fact, there have always been rich families there. One of the earliest lessons impressed upon me was that natural resources are a small factor in determining the wealth of a people or a family. The spirit and thrift of a city are much greater factors in making prosperity than are natural resources. The latter are worthless unless the people are imbued with a desire to create, and save, and study fundamentals. Those who have this desire can succeed even though they lack the natural advantages. Hence, my people accepted the rocky shores and turned them into quarries; they erected dams between the hills and made ice ponds; they went out on the briny deep and caught mackerel, haddock, cod, and Georges halibut. As a result men became rich in the granite business, in the ice business, and in the fish business.

Industries and banks grew up in the city. Good stores catered to the merchandising wants of the community. Yes, Gloucester was busy in those days with a population of about 25,000. It is a fine city to-day and in some respects it is more active, since its industries are more varied because manufacturing is gradually developing. Every visit to that city has taught me some lessons, and the past week has been no exception. It is the thoughts that have come to me during recent visits which I desire in this last chapter to pass on to you readers.

One of the most sobering thoughts is that practically all of the rich families of my boyhood days have since lost their money. The city then had its aristocracy, the same as Boston, Philadelphia, or Baltimore. It still has its well-to-do families, but they are of an entirely different group. Most of the beautiful homes of my boyhood days have been sold for boarding houses or for commercial purposes. In some cases the old folks have died and only the children survive; but in many cases the father or the mother is still living. Some of these families still live in the same old house, but the blinds are broken, the fence is tumbling down, tall grass and weeds are growing in what was once a beautiful garden, and the appearance of the place most graphically tells of the family tragedy.

This morning I have been up and down Main Street, Middle Street, and Prospect Street, looking up those places that I so revered in boyhood days. Men who had great businesses when I was a boy, with ships sailing all over the world, have broken down physically and financially. Their wives and daughters at home are doing their own work and struggling to make both ends meet.

These men cannot blame the city for their change in circumstances. If, to-day, no one had money in Gloucester it might be blamed on the rocks, bushes, cold winters, or treacherous sea. The fact is, however, that while these old families have been gradually tottering and disintegrating, other families that were unknown in my boyhood days have been gradually coming to the front. There is more wealth to-day in my birthplace than there ever was, but it is possessed by a new set of people. The rich boy who had the ponies and lived in the big house on the hill is now struggling with a little business or working for a meagre wage to keep his wife and family going. The poor boy of forty years ago, who used to sell papers and come to school barefooted, is carrying on the business of to-day. In fact, a large part of the business is being carried on to-day by Italians, Greeks, Portuguese, and other immigrants who had never seen this country when I was a youngster.

What does this mean to you, my readers? Whether you are rich or poor, it should mean much. If you are in good circumstances, it means that — unless you carefully heed fundamentals — the probabilities are that you will die poor. If your wife and children are able now to have all the things they want, it means that — unless you beware — probably they will some day have to struggle for the bare necessities of life. On the other hand, if you are in humble circumstances but are industrious, thrifty, and a student of fundamental business conditions, you and they may enjoy great prosperity in years to come. This does not mean that all rich men will die poor, or that all poor men will die rich. *It does mean that the families now on top must struggle to keep from going to the bottom, and the families at the bottom may easily rise to the top. It means that it is more difficult to conserve a business after it is created than it is to create it; and that it is more difficult to retain a fortune, than to accumulate one.*

What broke these rich families and caused their businesses to go to pieces? The answer is very simple. It is that these men knew the fishing business, the granite business, the ice business or were good merchants; but they failed to understand the fundamentals of business. They were industrious and thrifty only. When they happened to be working with a favorable tide of the business trend, they were prosperous and made a lot of money. But knowing nothing of such fundamentals, they failed to recognize the new conditions when the tide turned. They knew nothing about the four great periods of the business phase, and they never knew in which period they were. Consequently, when the tide of business turned, instead of changing their old methods and adopting new methods for the new phase of business, they continued in the same old way.

Some Gloucester friends went through the bankruptcy court, some merely assigned in favor of their creditors, and others simply petered out. With very few exceptions the business of every one of them is gone to-day. In some cases the business is being carried on by others, but in many cases the old wharves are not used, the old quarries are idle, and the farms are being cut up for the summer visitors. Old concerns when failing often have so much indebtedness that the once bare-footed boy can better afford to build a new wharf, open a new quarry, or start a new business for himself and by himself, than to take over the old wreck with its mortgages and indebtedness.

History continually repeats itself. Statistics clearly show that almost all successful businesses have been started either in a cellar or in a garret. Very few successful businessses of to-day started under auspicious circumstances. Very few have built on the ruins of other businesses. The great businesses of to-day started yesterday in the most humble way; and the great businesses of tomorrow are to-day being operated in cellars and garrets. Some look down upon the Greek fruit dealer, the Italian contractor, and the Jew tailor; but let me say that these Greeks, Italians, and Jews may be the great business men of the next generation. Unless very careful, you and your children will be working for them. They are very likely to be the bank presidents of our great cities, the owners of our large department stores and the captains of industry in 1950.

The wheel of opportunity is constantly revolving. It is very easy for those who are now on the top to be swept off when a change takes place in the great fundamental tide of business. It is a comparatively easy thing for those who happened to get onto the wheel at the right point of the business trend to make money owing to a change in the tide over which they have no control. These men, if they are industrious and honest, cannot help being successful for ten or twenty years. However, for a man to get on the wheel and stay on the wheel through the periods of over-expansion, decline, depression, and improvement is a great task that very few have the foresight and patience to accomplish. The reason is that business men do not understand fundamental conditions. Many of them do not know about business trends; others fail to recognize their effect upon them; and very few are willing to change their methods when the change comes in fundamental conditions.

Mind you, I do not say that these trend movements must continue indefinitely or that these waves during the coming years need be as severe as they are at present. Business could get along without them just as an individual can get along without being sick if he will govern himself in accordance with the basic laws of health.

Dissipation, however, is always followed by its headache and recuperation period, and as long as business continues to go on recurring sprees of over-inflation, we must expect the inevitable and equivalent reaction of deflation and hard times. You cannot ignore the law of Action and Reaction any more than you can ignore the law of gravitation.

Of course in some cases property has been dissipated by heedless children. In a few instances certain catastrophes have taken place for which the owners were not to blame. In 90 per cent. of the cases, however, the successful families of the last generation would still control the business interests of their city, if they had only known fundamentals and changed their methods when fundamental con-

ditions changed. The truth is that they unconsciously rode to success with the tide, and when the
tide went out they were left stranded on the beach.

Hence, I appeal to the business men of to-day to
avoid these pitfalls into which our predecessors have
fallen. Business disasters are no more necessary
than are cholera or smallpox scourges. There is no
need of business failures. To have new families
succeed it is not necessary for old families to fail.
Business opportunities in America have not yet been
scratched. Greater opportunities exist in every community. The old families of the past generation
should still be successful and have even greater
businesses to-day than they ever had. At the same
time there are opportunities for other families also
to climb up the ladder and be successful.

There never was a time when there were so many
opportunities for those who have the " Six I's of
Success "; namely, Integrity, Industry, Intelligence,
Initiative, Intensity, and Inspiration. But for any
business man to permanently succeed from now on
he must be a student of fundamental conditions and
guide his business by statistics as a sea captain guides
his ship by a chart.

COSIMO is an innovative publisher of books and publications that inspire, inform and engage readers worldwide. Our titles are drawn from a range of subjects including health, business, philosophy, history, science and sacred texts. We specialize in using print-on-demand technology (POD), making it possible to publish books for both general and specialized audiences and to keep books in print indefinitely. With POD technology new titles can reach their audiences faster and more efficiently than with traditional publishing.

> ➢ **Permanent Availability:** Our books & publications never go out-of-print.

> ➢ **Global Availability:** Our books are always available online at popular retailers and can be ordered from your favorite local bookstore.

COSIMO CLASSICS brings to life unique, rare, out-of-print classics representing subjects as diverse as *Alternative Health, Business and Economics, Eastern Philosophy, Personal Growth, Mythology, Philosophy, Sacred Texts, Science, Spirituality* and much more!

COSIMO-on-DEMAND publishes your books, publications and reports. If you are an Author, part of an Organization, or a Benefactor with a publishing project and would like to bring books back into print, publish new books fast and effectively, would like your publications, books, training guides, and conference reports to be made available to your members and wider audiences around the world, we can assist you with your publishing needs.

Visit our website at www.cosimobooks.com to learn more about Cosimo, browse our catalog, take part in surveys or campaigns, and sign-up for our newsletter.

And if you wish please drop us a line at info@cosimobooks.com. We look forward to hearing from you.